I'M GLAD YOU ASKED ME THAT

Foreword by Terence O'Rourke

'This isn't just a political memoir; it's gossip, grit and gas all rolled into one. You'll laugh, you'll wince, and you'll definitely learn something you didn't know. A fascinating cultural chronicle.

Terry Prone has lived a life at the centre of Irish politics and media, and she tells it the way only she can: sharp, hilarious and a little bit savage. *I'm Glad You Asked Me That* isn't weighed down with reverence or spin. It's full of jaw-dropping stories, insider chaos and the kind of honesty that makes you want to keep reading "just one more chapter". It's political history told with a wink and a sting – and I loved every page.'

Stefanie Preissner

I'M GLAD YOU ASKED ME THAT

The Political Years

Terry Prone

Published by
Red Stripe Press
Dublin
Ireland
email: info@redstripepress.com
www.redstripepress.com

© Terry Prone, 2025

Hardback ISBN 978-1-78605-272-8
Paperback ISBN 978-1-78605-280-3
ePub ISBN 978-1-78605-273-5

Every reasonable effort has been made to secure permission for the use of all photographs in this book. If you can identify any omissions or errors please notify the publishers, who will rectify the situation at the earliest opportunity.

A catalogue record for this book is available from the British Library. All rights reserved. No part of this publication may be reproduced, stored in a retrieval system or transmitted in any form or by any means, electronic, mechanical, photocopying, recording or otherwise, without the prior, written permission of the publisher.

This book is sold subject to the condition that it shall not, by way of trade or otherwise, be lent, resold, hired out, or otherwise circulated without the publisher's prior consent in any form of binding or cover other than that in which it is published and without a similar condition including this condition being imposed on the subsequent purchaser.

Printed in the EU

For Rose Hynes, without whom it would be lost in Texas

Acknowledgments

A wonderful meeting with Bill Fitzgerald, the Marine who was never a Marine, in Manhattan in 2025 reminded me of so much of the expansion years of our company and I am grateful to him and his family.

Máire Geoghegan-Quinn verified some personal details, corrected a serious error and – as always – was funny and helpful.

Barry McLoughlin, Head of Client Engagement and Senior Consultant at the Communications Clinic, made significant editorial recommendations which were slavishly followed.

Jonathan Williams, my agent, has for decades been a good friend to me and Tom, and relentlessly supportive of my work.

Michael Brennan brought his usual enthusiasm to the book, and Eileen O'Brien guided the manuscript through its various stages with speed, precision and generosity.

Seán O'Rourke and Pat Farrell were infinitely knowledgeable resources. Vincent Browne offered corrections and observations which were enormously helpful.

Despite being in the throes of post-production on the BBC/RTÉ production of *The Walsh Sisters*, Stefanie Preissner found the time to read the manuscript and comment on it. I'm grateful.

Foreword

I'm Glad You Asked Me That is a marvellous rendering of Terry Prone and Tom Savage's professional career. (Spoiler alert, Terry and Tom never advised politicians to use the 'I am glad you asked me that' response in any interview, ever.)

As someone whose first training course with Tom and Terry was in 1977, and who since got dipped more than a few times in Carr and, latterly, Communications Clinic training, it is a powerful reminder of some simple and memorable lessons in good communication that I and many others have benefited from over the years.

These lessons are told here through the lens of her many interactions with leading politicians – which makes it all the more fascinating. And for those curious about all those stories of Terry and Tom being at the centre of much of the most pivotal events in Irish politics over the last 50 or so years, the book doesn't disappoint. It's all here – from Charlie Haughey to Albert Reynolds, the apparently imperious but intriguing P. Flynn, the mercurial and courageous John O'Connell and the Gráinne Mhaol that is Máire Geoghegan-Quinn. And Terry is not exclusionary in her party political insights – she and Tom have provided advice to eight taoisigh and at least five political parties – so this book is deeply political yet uniquely un-party-political.

The book reminds us of the great enduring rule at the heart of Terry's communications training – above all else, be interesting, understandable and memorable (and it reveals how, despite her best efforts, not all of her political trainees were able to stick to that guidance).

So fasten your seatbelts and prepare to be whisked along, in impeccable and highly readable prose, to understand Terry's unique insight into some of the most consequential political events in our lifetime. It's a rip-roaring read – tasty and very satisfying.

Terence O'Rourke
Chair of the RTÉ Board

Contents

Foreword		vii
1	'Stop the Lights!'	1
2	Strangers in an RTÉ Car Park	11
3	Handlers and Propositions	21
4	Concentrating on Losing Money	29
5	Crossing Colonel Gaddafi's Rug	41
6	Tips and Tricks	59
7	Political Communications Move Centre Stage	67
8	Lochinvar	75
9	The Drift	86
10	The Woman Who Made Seán Doherty Tell the Truth	94
11	Haughey's Successor	115
12	Body Language, Lies and Crisis	128
13	Blackmail	135
14	A Great, Rainy Day	145
15	Here's Your Martello Tower	154
16	When Politicians Fall Out with One Another	165
17	Sure They're All the Same	173
Bibliography		180
Index		182

1

'STOP THE LIGHTS!'

It was the Swinging Sixties. Sex, drugs and rock and roll. For some teenagers, but not for me. I was having a great time in a quite different area. I'd started to appear on television at thirteen, in 1963, quickly moving from being a panellist on *Teen Talk* to becoming a regular in the same role on *The Late Late Show*. By sixteen, I also had my own radio programme and was writing for newspapers. As well as going to school. School was the only bad bit in an otherwise happy life.

Because I was visible, I became the voice of the younger generation, constantly invited to comment on matters of moment, about most of which I knew nothing. That included politics. We argued about almost everything else in our house: the priest's sermon at Sunday Mass; the quality of a book; 'Psycho', the driver of the 44A bus; and the space programmes of the USSR. Politics not so much.

The first politician I ever met was Garret FitzGerald, and I met him because the two of us were separately interviewed in a television programme made for the 1966 commemoration of 1916. It was, if I remember rightly, a joint BBC Northern Ireland and RTÉ production. I thought Garret was fascinating in his interview, not that I understood much of what he said. It was a bit like what Mark Twain said when his wife tried to break him of swearing by taking up the habit herself. Twain told her she had the words right but not the tune. I loved Garret's tune but had little grasp of what the words added up to. He stayed to watch my interview being recorded and was complimentary to my mother about me. My mother, who thought Fine Gael was the best party in oratorical terms, was deadly chuffed.

The man who had first spotted me as having media potential, Bunny Carr, meanwhile, had achieved monumental national fame for himself. He put the phrase 'Stop the lights!' into the national lexicon with a quiz show called *Quicksilver* that was broadcast from virtually every townland in Ireland. Children in school who couldn't think of the answer to a teacher's question used it. His *Teen Talk* was followed by another programme involving young people who went on to become national figures. He was receiving black plastic sackfuls of fan mail every week and he was editing a page for an evening newspaper.

Then the assistant controller of programmes in RTÉ asked him if he'd like to present a weekly programme called *The Politicians*, telling him that the Fianna Fáil, Fine Gael and Labour parties had been asked if they were all right with him as presenter and had said yes. Looking back, it seems extraordinary that the three main parties would be asked for their opinion, never mind their permission, on a prospective presenter. Yet, in the mid-sixties, it wasn't just that they were asked; they were asked before the idea was even floated past the prospective presenter. Furthermore, the contradictions in the sequence didn't even strike him. That was partly because the Oireachtas was a constant pain in the arse to the early RTÉ TV producers and presenters and partly, too, because Bunny was so eager to drag Irish politicians into the television age. Since Irish TV had started, he believed they had failed to come to terms with it. 'They recognise and mostly exaggerate its influence,' he said. 'They feel they should be in there doing something and are also aware of the two-edged possibilities of success and failure on any programme.'

The chance to be the catalyst for change in this paralysing context appealed enormously to him. He also wanted to prove that you could be a 'heavyweight' interviewer without getting aggressive with your interviewees. It all made sense, as paving the road to hell always does.

The series was a disaster. Every week they locked Bunny in a studio with a Fianna Fáil, a Fine Gael and a Labour backbencher, where he presented them with viewers' questions the politicians had not seen in advance.

'Week after week, I met three reasonable men in the conference room,' he later wrote. 'Then they went into a studio and "performed". They had a competition to see which of them could, with maximum number of clichés, regurgitate their party's line on any given subject. They scored off each other like bold schoolboys.'

It's worth pointing out two things at this point. The first is that no women were present. Only a handful of TDs were women at the time, many if not most of them widows continuing to hold their husbands' seats, almost none of them considered by their parties as worth offering to a TV programme, even if it was presented by nice, mild Bunny Carr. The second is that scoring points off each other like bold schoolchildren didn't die off with the last century; the behaviour Bunny noted continues to this day. They displayed arrogance, shrewdness, ignorance and contempt in equal portions. Never once in eighteen months did I hear any of them say 'I don't know'. If you 'don't know' in broadcasting you have a choice. You can either say you don't or you can prove you don't.

Too often, his panellists took the second option and interest in them waned as a result of the consequent waffle. Bunny would always accompany the programme participants afterwards to a pub close to Nutley Lane, where RTÉ lived (and still lives). Sooner or later, when a couple of pints had been sunk, one of them would snigger triumphantly, 'Mind you, you didn't get much outa me, now, did you?' Mystified, Bunny would ask them why they concentrated on not being interesting in the studio when, in many, although not all, cases, they were capable of being remarkably interesting. They told him, with what he interpreted as 'a certain trace of contempt for their supporters', that 'the punters expect it'. As Bunny saw it:

They were dead wrong. That series began with a high TAM [TV audience measurement] rating and crashed into oblivion in the low twenties. The plain people of Ireland switched the thing off. I don't blame them. They had been insultingly underestimated by their servants who thought playing games would fill bellies of a nation hungry for political food.

Ironically, the television disaster that was *The Politicians* did the politicians themselves no harm and did the presenter no favours. Because they made infrequent appearances, none of the politicians, as individuals, were blamed for the boredom it generated, whereas Bunny was there every week, looking less and less happy as time went on. Fair-mindedly, Bunny did admit that the Irish audience is a particularly difficult one, being 'devious' and always looking behind a factual statement made by a politician to see what they are really getting at. 'It's extremely difficult [for politicians]', he admitted. 'It's about winning an honest hearing rather than defeating an opponent.'

Bunny's career shifted away from such concerns when he left RTÉ, although with great resentment over the comfort manifested by his bosses at the prospect of his exit. For a few years, he served as a top executive in the Industrial Development Authority, before being wooed back into an aspect of broadcasting by a priest named Father Joe Dunn, who had been sent to the US by the hierarchy to learn the secrets of media training so that the Catholic Church in Ireland could equip its officer class to perform on the medium they could see was going to be enormously powerful.

Joe Dunn persuaded Bunny Carr to head up the Catholic Communications Centre at the top of Booterstown Avenue, where Carr quickly recruited Father Tom Savage, a sociologist who showed up frequently on UTV's religious programming, and a former RTÉ producer named Barry Baker. The three of them were kept busy for several years training priests, sisters and brothers in media skills – with the help of Father Brian D'Arcy, who led the written skills training – and, in the process, developed an understanding of just how different American media skills were from what the Irish market required.

America believed that appearance was crucial. The contrast between the haggard, unshaven Richard Nixon in a shirt too big for him, debating with a younger, tanned John F. Kennedy had imprinted itself on American media consciousness, fitting neatly into existing preconceptions. One American presidential candidate had, after all, been selected as a candidate without reference to his intelligence or capabilities, of which he had none, but based only on him looking presidential and being tall. Tall mattered more than clever. A lot more. American presidents have, for the most part, been markedly taller than the average US citizen. Starting from that point and adding instructions to smile at the end of your sentences stunted American media training for politicians to such an extent that it wasn't until 1984 that a major politician – former Vice-President Walter Mondale – blamed losing the presidential race on his lack of television skills.

Media training in Ireland was developed by Bunny Carr and Tom Savage without much reference to what was going on in America, for the good reason that Irish media was different. There was more of it, for starters. Local newspapers were enormously powerful, arriving once a week and sitting for familial consumption on a coffee table for the following seven days until scrunched into fire-starting material. Although local radio was not yet a factor, Radio Éireann was changing fast, even without competition. For decades, radio, coming only from RÉ's Henry Street studios, was something that happened early in the morning, disappeared mid-morning, returned at lunchtime, nodded off again mid-afternoon and returned in time to give listeners the evening news. In the mid-sixties, a big celebration was staged when radio went 'round the clock', although that didn't include any serious attention to the night-time hours.

Irish television, arriving in the early sixties, quickly became a national obsession, with Telefís Éireann seen as being more important as you moved westwards. On the east coast, it was possible to access BBC, albeit in a somewhat snowy form.

Despite the increased reach of radio and TV, political programming was limited. Backbenchers got little airtime, which made Bunny even madder over their failure to profit from his offering. Frontbenchers were interviewed about aspects of their portfolios. Those interviews were conducted with respect in a context where major corruption was not suspected and issues like the arms trial were in the future. They were, nonetheless, as boring as hell.

Bunny Carr and Tom Savage wanted to change that. Arguably, Tom understood local politics better than Bunny. His parents were passionate followers of Fine Gael and Fianna Fáil, each voting in every general election to cancel out the vote of the other. His brother Peter was and still is a Fianna Fáil councillor in Louth, whose best pal in politics was a Fine Gael colleague. Tom was a sociologist with some understanding of group affiliation and a fascination with the different patois of the three main parties. He maintained that a transcript of five minutes from any one of their members would be identifiable at a glance as coming from that party, so specific was the party influence on the words used.

It was Tom who divided the audience for a political communication into three.

- First were the people who were on the politician's side before they opened their mouth. You don't need to aim at them; it's a waste of your time.
- Second were the folk whose loyalties belonged elsewhere. Aiming at them is also a waste of your time because their identity resides in being opposed to you.
- Third were the group who hadn't made up their minds. They, and only they, were to be focused on.

The first of those three was the biggest stumbling block for politicians, who were convinced that the guarantee of excellence was when a party loyalist praised them for uttering some favoured mantra that meant damn all to anybody other than the already converted. It took a lot of training to get many of those early backbenchers to focus on the people who actually elected them. Concentrating on what Bunny and Tom always called 'the floating voter' took a lot of practice but was key to a set of principles drawn from training religious, one of which was that the voter was regarded as singular. Television couldn't cope with a politician who, in an interview, seemed to be addressing the entire nation. It was too intimate a medium for that back-of-the-lorry stuff. Plus, those who behaved as if a cross-section of the country was paying attention to them tended needlessly to elevate their locution, reaching into the written word, with its longer sentences and conceptual language, rather than staying in the spoken word, which they regarded as somehow cheaper and less impressive.

It was relatively easy to get the religious past that hurdle. All any trainer had to do was use the gospels as an example of perfectly simple, indelibly memorable communication. The 'gotcha' reaction was immediately visible. Plus the clergy had been instructed by their bosses to get their media act together.

No Irish political leaders had issued a parallel instruction, and so the troops on the ground were less motivated, coming more slowly to the realisation that the three requirements of TV and radio were that you be interesting, understandable and memorable. Miss out on any one of the three and viewers wouldn't recall or act on your communication, which established that you might as well have stayed in bed. In order to be all three, you had to offer pictures, stories and examples, rather than general statements. Not a difficult task, you might think, for a race whose culture had, for a millennium, been exclusively oral.

But as Bunny had found to his cost, politicians who, with a few pints in them, were full of vivid yarns, were vastly different in a TV studio, where they talked like a party manifesto made human. Or nearly human. They were reaching for a performance that had nothing to do with who they really were, greatly helped by pals within the party who believed they should be 'statesmanlike'. That's a deadly one. The minute anybody strives to be statesmanlike they become boring, pompous and wooden. But they're always willing to try because so many of them are convinced that their real self isn't good enough. Which is why too much of what now presents as media training is essentially an avoidance of authenticity: Be more relatable/punchy/authoritative, but whatever you do, don't be yourself.

It was Tom who taught all of us in our first company and, later, in The Communications Clinic, to casually interrogate our trainees by asking them questions about their experience of sport or their family or how their first name was chosen. They would talk. They would relax. They would tell funny stories. They would explain their lives. They would be authentic. Whenever possible, we would quietly record them before we did an 'official' recording to capture them being the best of themselves.

'We're actually in the transport business,' Tom would tell us. 'Great training is capturing people when they're communicating naturally and helping them to transport that into the pressured situation of a platform or studio.'

That takes time. It takes commitment on the part of the course participant. It's much easier to put words in their mouths, teach them to answer a query with the lie, 'I'm glad you asked me that question' and tell them to smile at the end of their sentences. Much easier. But profoundly dishonest.

Fortunately, when Bunny and Tom started to develop media skills training, they were the first and only option. The first into any market has an enormous advantage. Politicians heard that the Catholic Communications Centre was running 'open courses' that anybody could attend, and some of them booked a place on one of those monthly courses, which turned out to be doubly useful to them because of the insights they gained from other participants who had neither knowledge of, nor much interest in, party politics.

Honestly, though, it was kind of a miracle that any politicians ever made this gain. Neither Tom nor Bunny nor any of the other Centre staff knew the first thing about marketing. Because the Catholic hierarchy, from the outset, fatally refused to invest in its own venture, Bunny was forced to try to find what are nowadays called alternative income streams. He was lousy at it. Monthly courses were held, but publicised in advance? Never. Bunny and Tom had two disabling business characteristics. They preferred training over the task of selling it to anybody, for one thing, and for another, the two of them hated the word 'profit'. (Although I was equally ignorant about marketing, I wasn't that involved at the time, appearing now and again as a guest lecturer/assessor and no more than that.)

Here's the sad part, from a business point of view. Word of mouth about the open courses was good. So, even without advertising or PR support, people rang up, looking to join one of the three-day courses. Neither Tom nor Bunny had ever heard of 'surrender business', but that's what it was: customers literally arrived wanting to pay money. That was great, except that there was never enough of them. The course could take two streams of seven. It rarely got to even one full stream. Surrender business will only go so far. So clueless was Bunny – despite being a former banker and a one-time director of the IDA – that as soon as three paying customers pitched up for an open course, he was quite happy to make up the remainder of the seven by 'papering the house', giving complimentary places to others. The complimentary participants usually outnumbered the paying customers, but it was interpreted as long-term strategic marketing.

The Catholic hierarchy had damn all interest in long-term strategic marketing and the moment Father Tom Savage announced that he was leaving the priesthood, they told Bunny Carr to fire him, which he refused to do, on the basis that his skills were not affected by his prospective laicisation. The bishops promptly halved the Communications Centre budget, giving Bunny an incentive to leave and set up his own communications consultancy. He had never wanted to do this, but he didn't have much choice.

The records of politicians participating in open courses in the Catholic Communications Centre have long disappeared. However, it is a measure of how low political training sat in our priorities at the time that no one could ever remember who those early political visitors were. Bunny set up his new business in Orwell Road, in premises leased from the Dominicans. Tom and I concentrated on surviving through freelance journalism. Bunny persuaded an old pal of his, Hugh McGowan, a Bank of Ireland bank manager in Marino, to give us a mortgage on the dodgy basis that 'These people have no money right now, but they will make money. Trust me on this.' Hugh did, and we made the payments every month. We might not have had furniture, other than the bed Tom brought with him, but we were on the long route to owning our own home.

When, one Stephen's Day, Bunny arrived at our little house in Baldoyle to propose that we join him in turning what was then, in his words, a 'sheltered workshop' into a business, neither of us thought of politicians as a market Carr Communications should go after or be seen to specialise in. Ironic, given the level to which the brand later became associated with politics. That happened because of random interventions on the part of two men who may not even have known each other: Jack Lynch and John O'Connell.

2

Strangers in an RTÉ Car Park

Although, up to his Stephen's Day visit, we were not part of Bunny's new company, we were in constant touch with him. He had become godfather to our son Anton when we eventually got around to having the latter baptised. Anton was about six months old at the time, and wanted to play every role in the ceremony, particularly desiring to hold the candle. Bunny was in stitches, announcing that we definitely had a future broadcaster on our hands. (The priest's smile, on the other hand, was reminiscent of Garfield the cartoon cat wishing people a happy day 'someplace else'.)

The two of us were making a precarious living as freelance journalists, but Bunny frequently called on us to fill gaps, in that first year, which was fun and always unexpected. Tom was never fazed by the unexpected. You don't manage, as a curate in a country area near Crossmaglen during the Troubles, if you can't think on your feet. Constantly called out in the middle of the night to give the last rites to the injured or desperately ill, he would go back to the parochial house, undress and slump into so deep a sleep that only the position of his clothes the following morning clued him in as to how he had spent some of the night. On one occasion, tending to a man who had been knocked off his bicycle, he listened to the panicked predictions of the man holding a torch to light the injured man's face.

'He's on the way out, Father, God love him,' the torch-holder muttered. 'I've been askin' him who he is since I got here and not a word out of him. Definitely a goner.'

Tom listened, did his priestly task, and, as he and the torch-holder heard the ambulance siren approaching, looked once more at the bloodied face and the staring eyes of the injured man and snapped his fingers. Suddenly, he realised that he knew him and named him to the arriving paramedics, also telling them that the man would be fine.

'Don't worry that he doesn't respond to you,' he told them. 'He's profoundly deaf and mute.'

Tom was right. The man survived the accident without sequelae.

That ability to deal with and make sense of the new, combined with utter fearlessness, meant that when Bunny Carr phoned him in 1977 and asked him to abandon whatever he was doing and instead go immediately to RTÉ, Tom asked only a few questions. Who would he meet there? Jack Lynch, leader of Fianna Fáil. Why? Because Lynch was in RTÉ to do a party political broadcast and it wasn't going well. And? And Bunny, when the call came from Lynch asking if Bunny had someone who could rescue the situation, had immediately nominated Tom.

It was a measure of the trust between Bunny and Tom that the former trusted the latter to rescue a party political broadcast while knowing that the latter had never had hand, act or part in a party political up to that point. He did, however, know how to write for television and deliver pieces to camera, having for a couple of years been the most popular presenter of UTV's five-minute religious slot at the end of the day's broadcasting. Plus he was a great trainer. In this instance, he also had something in common with Jack Lynch. He was a talented sportsman. He played football, hurling and had won a Sigerson Cup medal for tennis.

T. Ryle Dwyer, for decades a contributor to the *Irish Examiner* and a historian too, called Lynch 'the most popular politician since

Daniel O'Connell'. But before that, Lynch had been a dual player of Gaelic games throughout the 1930s and 1940s. In total, he won eight Munster titles – six in hurling and two in football; six All-Irelands – five in hurling and one in football; and countless other testaments to his prowess. Because of his sporting fame, he was asked to run by more than one political party but started in politics as Fianna Fáil leader Éamon de Valera's speechwriter and researcher. From the fifties onwards, he was a TD, holding many parliamentary posts. In 1966, the leader of the party, Seán Lemass, resigned, ushering in a fraught leadership contest that led to deep and continuing rifts within the party. Lynch beat George Colley, the only survivor of a large field of aspirants, by 52 votes to 19, becoming leader in November of that year.

Following Bunny's phone call, Tom drove to what was then referred to as Montrose, where he found Jack Lynch in his car in the car park. He sat into the car with him while the armed garda driver sat in the back. Unhurried, always, in the face of a deadline or a crisis, Tom did what he always did with other sportsmen: talked about sport. The two of them bonded. Lynch relaxed. Then Tom asked him to tell him what the problem was and learned that one of the participants in the broadcast, one Charles J. Haughey, was refusing to be present in studio when Lynch was there. Haughey and Lynch were daggers drawn on a permanent basis unrelated to the party political. So? asked Tom. Haughey was going to have to be filmed separately. Fine. Lynch was resigned to that. What was seriously worrying him was the script he had been handed, and once Tom saw it, he was equally worried. Out came the fountain pen and Tom started to edit and rewrite the script, lining up the pages on the dashboard. When he handed it to Lynch, the Fianna Fáil leader read the beautiful cursive handwriting with ease and nodded at the entirety of it: no argument with any of what Tom called the 'emendations'.

Tom told Lynch to stay put and went into the main building in Donnybrook, still shiny and new at that point, and talked with the camera operators. It would be difficult to amend the autocue script at this time, one of them pointed out. Not necessary, Tom responded, having formed the idea that the programme should be filmed outside the studio, with the exception of Haughey's bit. This, it was pointed out to him, had never happened before.

From their ignoble beginnings, party political broadcasts were a black and white nightmare featuring the incompetent reading the incomprehensible off an unfamiliar technology, standing at a podium that made them look like they'd recently been convicted of serial killing. Tom invited the RTÉ lads, who knew him from a few years' appearances on the late-night tiny sermon slot broadcast by the station (called *Outlook*) to consider how much more rewarding it would be to work outside, without autocue. They were more than open to the proposition. Cameras were hoisted up, tripods carried and the crew set up afresh around Lynch's car.

Lynch himself had been quietly working his way through the amended script and told Tom he was ready. Tom walked him through it. Lynch would talk to the camera through the window of the car and when he reached the end of it, would smack the door of the car as a signal to his driver, now back in the seat beside him, to get the Merc moving. Tom explained to Lynch that many takes would probably be needed, but the first – although it was going to be filmed – would be just a run-through. Lynch nodded, accepted instructions about countdowns, turned to the camera as if it was an old friend, talked to it, smacked the car door and was taken off down the RTÉ drive. It might have been intended as a rehearsal but it was a perfect take. The crew nodded: it would insert into the final programme beautifully, they predicted, and it did. Everybody was happy.

The only person who came badly out of that party political was Charles Haughey, who delivered a solidly stilted piece to camera in the middle of an otherwise lively short programme. He was like a dead man talking to camera in the RTÉ studio. It did Haughey no favours, but – as the embattled always do – he learned the wrong lesson from it. Instead of figuring that this Tom Savage person had managed to make Jack Lynch look energetic and persuasive, CJ simply decided that Tom, whom he had never met, belonged in the enemy camp. The word went out within Fianna Fáil even before Lynch departed the leadership: do not go near Carr Communications.

Gossip about Haughey's hatred of us reached us. While we knew that CJ, as Machiavelli noted of Louis XII of France, 'esteemed no one unless that person was armed or had something to give', low esteem didn't seem to describe his loathing for us. It was the first time we had encountered the tribal resistance to communications skills building. As far as we were concerned, we were in the business of training people, including politicians, to express themselves through mass media in a way that was interesting, understandable and memorable. We were in the business of forcing politicians to find good examples for the concepts they (or their expert advisers) adduced, so that listeners and viewers could grasp the meaning at first hearing. None of that required us to share the opinions of the politician in front of us, and most of the time we didn't. We were not selling tattooed affinity. We were selling skills. Down through the following decades, we worked, at different times, for Fianna Fáil, Fine Gael, Labour, the Green Party and the Progressive Democrats, as well as for Northern Ireland and overseas politicians. Eventually a political party decided to pay us enough to exclusively retain our services, but that was much later.

Meanwhile, that couple of hours in sunshine in the grounds of RTÉ won Tom Savage a reputation as a man who had a unique take on party political broadcasts, and so, in subsequent years, our company became the go-to place for almost all political parties to seek advice on or production of party political broadcasts, than which no more pointless task has ever been invented. Party political broadcasts are a uniquely Irish waste of time, about which we get ludicrously virtuous because, while other countries allow their political candidates to pay big money to be made look credible by good TV production, we insist on a format that makes almost everybody look equally bad and makes no measurable contribution, ever, to the electoral result. Tom's direction of the Lynch party political broadcast resulted in something that was at best okay to look at, with the exception of the Charles Haughey section, which he delivered with all the forced gravity of a judge announcing a death sentence. None of which caused or contributed to Jack Lynch's party winning a landslide victory on that occasion. That was delivered through shocking promises made by Fianna Fáil, which have haunted them and the nation pretty much ever since. Haughey and his people had no justification for hating our company, but, as a group, they could work up a good hate in a minute, with or without supporting evidence. In addition to the Jack Lynch hatred, bad and all as that was, Dr Garret FitzGerald later made no secret of the fact that he had been prepped for major TV appearances by Bunny Carr, which exacerbated Fianna Fáil's loathing of the company.

As soon as Haughey became leader of Fianna Fáil, therefore, the word went out to frontbenchers and backbenchers alike: put not a foot in Carr Communications, which Tom and I had joined when Bunny decided he had to move from running something that was, as he put it, 'halfway between a sheltered workshop and a cottage industry' to running a big business and he would need the two of us to help him achieve it. Haughey's ban didn't actually stop them coming, of course. It just meant that they came at odd hours and parked their cars around the back of the Old Railway Station on Taney Road, Dundrum, where we had moved when the borrowed premises in Orwell Road became too small. The Fianna Fáil members who came to us on the sly told us that Haughey had built a TV studio out in Kinsealy and that Don Lydon, the psychologist based in St John of God's (later a Fianna Fáil senator) did all the training out there. We never found out how true or false this was.

The other man who was instrumental in making us synonymous with political communication was Dr John O'Connell. John, who never played sport of any kind, grew up in poverty in the centre of Dublin. He was lucky to survive his childhood. Three of his siblings didn't, succumbing to TB, or 'galloping consumption', in their teens. It made no sense for John, as a teenager, to decide he was going to be a doctor. Medicine was at the time an almost generational career, running in families. Families who were rich, or at least 'comfortable', neither of which was where John was situate. He got neither help nor encouragement from anyone. In fact, he met with direct opposition and contempt, particularly for his footwear, which consisted of squeaky plastic sandals, worn summer and winter because they were all he could afford. But neither opposition nor the contempt that scarred him were going to stop him. He got together the money he needed by working as a bookie's tout, entered medical school and aced every exam before setting up as a GP infused with the determination to become rich. Rich was where he was going and the quicker he could put behind him any association with the grinding poverty of his youth the better. Until a Jewish doctor colleague shocked him into an acceptance that he should be the GP of the Dublin slums, which he managed to do while coming up with new publications, including MIMS, in 1960. MIMS, the *Monthly Index of Medical Specialities*, contains impartial information on drugs available for prescription in Ireland. That made him a fortune. His weekly newspaper, the *Irish Medical Times*, made him a second fortune.

John's work in the slums made him a beloved figure referred to by everybody as Dr John. But it also rooted in him a conviction, amply supported by public health statistics, then and now, that to be poor was to be condemned to poor health, no matter what you tried to do to ensure a different outcome. Gradually, he came to the conclusion that, along with his twin careers, he needed another. He needed to get into politics. With his distinctive determination, he joined the Labour Party and nailed a seat as a Dáil deputy.

That was where he first became widely regarded as impossible. He had no patience for process or the people who espoused it. He had no time for postponement or the people who used it to delay the delivery of what he considered essentials. Except in medicine, he had little interest in details and would get furious with anyone – even those close to him – who tried to explain the subtlety of issues he saw as crystal clear and binary. He saw treachery on all sides, except, peculiarly, in people he might not have been expected to get along with or trust. He entered partnerships with British Conservative MPs that lasted for years and delivered mutual profit. He became the Irish representative for a number of Saudi sheiks who were into horse breeding, on which he became an expert. The boy whose mother could not read ended up owning several Mercedes from the fleet of the Sultan of Brunei and having his own driver, to allow him to work in the car.

Sheikhs and MPs might stay pals with Dr John O'Connell, but colleagues in the Labour Party did not. He quickly came to the view that individuals like Brendan Corish were placeholders who had little in the way of what he regarded as socialist philosophy. He viewed party performance on several of his key issues – including holding the makers of the Thalidomide drug to account – as pathetic and gutless. He was a constant thorn in the side of the party he espoused and eventually he walked out on it.

I had been in sporadic contact with John from the time I ghost-wrote his autobiography, and wasn't surprised when he left Labour. I misread him, though, making the wrong assumption that he would continue in politics as an Independent. Not so. He rang me one day to warn me that the evening news would carry a report about him joining Fianna Fáil, where Jack Lynch had been succeeded by Charles Haughey.

Fianna Fáil was riven with hatred and distinguished, at the time, by a level of corruption that was glimpsed by the population, but – like Haughey's extra-marital relationship with journalist Terry Keane – was kept in the Nudge Nudge, Say Nothing box.

It is difficult to portray that corruption and complicit silence today, just as it's difficult to portray the level of alcoholism that distinguished the politics of the time, which saw younger politicians doing fireman's lifts on colleagues who were unconscious, covered in puke and urine in the Dáil bar, and getting them to their Dublin homes. It was just the way it was.

Mass media accepted most of it. Nobody in media baulked at the notion that the mistress of a prime minister could hawk their weekly encounters pseudonymously through a Sunday newspaper, just as few in media tried to nail down the first-names-and-favours methodology by which state directorships and public service contracts were awarded. We in Carr Communications learned early on that one particular public affairs consultant closely linked to Fianna Fáil backhanded his way to the majority of civil and public service contracts and that there was no point in going up against him unless we got into the bribery business too. We won enough business in the private sector to keep us going, and some government departments sent non-tender work our way, much of it in emergency situations after we developed a reputation as good advisers in a crisis.

With all that as an open secret, my dismay was enormous when John told me he had left the Labour Party and joined Fianna Fáil. How could he?

Over the course of a long phone call, it became clear that John adored Charlie Haughey. Haughey was successful, if you measured him by his Kinsealy residence and apparently limitless money. John believed that money came from Haughey's genius as an accountant. We know to the differ now. Rich men like Ben Dunne made themselves influential by stuffing cash into Haughey's eager hands. Quiet references to 'brown envelopes' were constant, but John dismissed my queries on that – it was just bad stuff being put about by envious begrudgers. Haughey, he swore to me, had a deep desire to fight poverty. (This was true: he fought off any threat of personal poverty with inspirational determination.) If I ever met Haughey's constituents from the poor areas, John told me fervently, I would understand. They were so grateful to him.

'Oh, right,' I said. 'The turkeys at Christmas.'

This was in reference to a story in *Hibernia*, the fortnightly review, about Haughey, lord-of-the-manor fashion, donating turkeys to impoverished households in his constituency coming up to Christmas. John sounded genuinely hurt by the sneer. Haughey was always available to help poor people, he told me, the hero-worship self-evident. Now, admittedly, the party, and even Haughey himself, had problems with the media. The leader needed to have Tom and me work on him and all would be well. I was startled into both contradiction and laughter, and he left that alone at the time, concentrating on becoming a good member of the Soldiers of Destiny and a faithful servant of the Master of Kinsealy. But it was a wish he didn't forget, and would revisit later. I was sad that John had made the move but it didn't change my affection for this deeply kind, phenomenally generous man.

3

Handlers and Propositions

If Fianna Fáil devoted itself to staying in power at all costs while fighting internal fights with a vengeance, from the mid-sixties Fine Gael and Labour seemed to hold the promise of a glamorous and idealistic future for politics.

The first indication of an understanding of the importance of communication or, more crudely, of 'image' creation came in the 1966 presidential election, when Fine Gael put Judge Tom O'Higgins up against the incumbent, Éamon de Valera. The age difference may have been the catalyst for the Fine Gael campaign: de Valera was eighty-three and looked every minute of it. O'Higgins was in his early fifties.

The visual impact of the O'Higgins campaign was pure Camelot, drawing on the romance associated with John F. Kennedy and his wife Jacqueline. O'Higgins, his wife and his seven children were photographed to present them as cool, attractive and modern. Who dreamed up the Camelot parallels is not easy to find out, but the formidable journalist and critic Emer O'Kelly served as communications adviser to the campaign. O'Higgins, early on, set out to schedule and attend more than a hundred meetings throughout the country, covering thousands of miles, sometimes attending multiple rallies per night. The message was inescapable: here was a dynamic Irish version of JFK, filled with energy and youth. They used planes to drop balloons. They enthralled political commentators. This was, as the highly regarded political commentator John Healy put it, Fine Gael with its tail up.

The problem for Fine Gael was de Valera. He might be, indeed he demonstrably was, old and weary, but he was still ruthlessly clever and came up with a killer stroke. He decided that, since he was already president, it would be beneath his dignity to campaign during this election as if he were a lowly non-incumbent candidate for the Oireachtas. There would be no interviews, no big debate with O'Higgins. That he got away with this is, in retrospect, astonishing. RTÉ caved in. The national broadcaster would not cover Dev's campaign, but, more important, neither would it, on the grounds of fairness, cover the O'Higgins campaign. This didn't obviate the President from appearing, as he continued to do, at events putting him in a good light, not as a candidate, but as the holder of the office. So while stymying O'Higgins by removing him from the national airwaves at a time when RTÉ had no competition, de Valera could continue to be a constant visual presence. It was genius.

Fine Gael – rightly but ineffectively – went crazy. Liam Cosgrave, the leader of Fine Gael, pointed out that it was unjust to continue to cover de Valera while excluding O'Higgins from TV and radio. He got nowhere. Indeed, things got worse. For the first time ever, Fianna Fáil engaged in private polling, which revealed that the Fine Gael candidate's profile and likeability were, from Fianna Fáil 's point of view, dangerously high. Dev upped the number of the public engagements that would be covered by RTÉ on the basis that it was the fiftieth anniversary year of 1916, in which he had played a signal part, which of course meant he had to be the link to that glorious rebellion. More crudely (but not that much more crudely) the Fianna Fáil minister for agriculture, Charles Haughey, announced less than a week before polling day that £5.5 million was going to farmers. In today's money, that would be €50 million.

Even with all that chicanery, O'Higgins was able to use Wellington's great description of the Battle of Waterloo, 'A damned close-run thing', to describe his eventual loss. It was not a rout. It was a tight result, with Dev making it back to the Áras by less than 11,000 votes nationally. It was, nonetheless, a harbinger of a new political interest in youth at a time of great change.

Charles Haughey became leader of Fianna Fáil, Garret FitzGerald became leader of Fine Gael and, despite competition from a handsome Cork man named Michael O'Leary, who was in his early fifties at the time and looked even younger, Frank Cluskey became Labour Party leader, although his time in the role was shortened when he lost his seat to Dr John O'Connell, the latter running as an Independent, having fallen out with Labour, in the 1981 general election, after which his party unanimously elected Michael O'Leary. All change.

Haughey called the 1981 election at a time of overwhelming Fianna Fáil popularity, only to have to postpone it because of the Stardust disaster, which saw teenagers from his constituency burned to death in a highly suspicious fire in the eponymous dance hall. The postponement drained the electoral impetus from his party, and the election moved him out of Government Buildings.

The Taoiseach's job went to Garret FitzGerald, who seemed to have pretty much everything going for him. He had a distinctive appearance and no vanity, as evidenced by his arrival at one event wearing mismatched shoes. His clever wife Joan was disabled and he managed her wheelchair like a pro – as well as deferring to her views. He talked in erudite bursts and articulated a less right-wing stance for Fine Gael than had traditionally been its preference, the new stance being greatly influenced by Declan Costello's paper *Towards a Just Society*. In addition, he had young, dynamic advisers who often travelled with him. People like Bill O'Herlihy, Pat Heneghan, Frank Flannery and party secretary Peter Prendergast. The last restructured the party in a way that, post factum, seemed commonsensical, as all quiet organisational revolutions do.

Although he concentrated on the internal workings of Fine Gael, I believe it was Prendergast who persuaded Garret that he needed to master television and that Bunny Carr was the man to help him do it, so it was at the beginning of the 1980s that our company began to work with FitzGerald.

It was a lot of fun, whatever about being productive. Garret would always arrive scattered and late. He once turned up in another company's studios, baffling and scaring the hell out of them. Getting him to stop talking and submit to an interview was always difficult, because he was an ideas man, engaged in a constant argument between sources. Bunny loved working with him, and the Young Turk advisers adopted a position as informational resources, staying silent except when asked for data. They saw Bunny seeking to reduce the complexity of what FitzGerald had to say, working hard to find concrete examples of the concepts with which the FitzGerald discourse was replete, going back over agreed courses of action so that Garret made more coherent speeches and walked into radio and TV studios with some sense of objective and something interesting to offer. It worked about 20 per cent of the time. Garret was infinitely distractable and intellectually undisciplined.

Paradoxically, even though we never claimed to have radically improved Garret's media skills, we gained great publicity from working with him. He was Garret the Good, in contrast to Charlie Haughey, who was not to be trusted and who looked at the world from under threateningly hooded eyes. Garret inspired a generation of Department of Foreign Affairs civil servants, who talked of him constantly, quoting principles they heard him adduce. (Some of them still do.) Journalists and broadcasters loved him too. He had no 'side' and was patently authentic. Even though broadcasters were instinctively suspicious of what we in the company did, they came to a strangely contradictory conclusion: it was obvious that we hadn't trained him to avoid answering tough questions (he never recognised an incoming tough question for what it was) or say things like 'I'm glad you asked me that question' or smile meaninglessly. But because he was likeable and knowledgeable on their programmes, they figured we must have done something good. It was around this time that our brand began to be associated with political training, and even though it never amounted to more than 3 per cent of our turnover, it created 90 per cent of the interest in us. Few journalists, with the notable exception of Liam Fay, ever submitted themselves as guinea pigs to the kind of training we did, but they all had theories about us, which positioned us somewhere between Machiavelli and a bad model agency.

This drove me nuts and I let it show until my mother ticked me off for being pompous and defensive. She quoted the axiom about no publicity being bad publicity, and she was right. This was in the ten-year period during which we made a yearly loss because none of us knew how to run a business. We couldn't afford to advertise or do any kind of marketing, although I did have the small white two-door Honda I drove dolled up in the company livery, which my husband truly hated. Not only did he flatly refuse ever to drive it, he also, when he pulled up on the path outside our little Baldoyle home, gave it a filthy look, every time, to punish it. It bothered him so much that I promised the replacement would be left unembellished, which, looking back, may not have been much of a consolation to him, since we weren't going to be able to afford a replacement for quite a while.

Our association with Garret the Good exacerbated the hatred Haughey faithful within Fianna Fáil harboured for us and grievously terrified the minority who sneaked up to our back door.

They were great years for political work because they were unstable years. John Bruton, who, like Garret, never saw a new idea he didn't want to research and adopt as party policy, was the Minister for Finance who introduced VAT on children's shoes for fear that grown women with small feet would get away with wearing kids' clobber. Even though Labour were in government, it was a left-wing Independent and a Workers' Party deputy who indicated they weren't having any of this. The infamous tax on children's shoes brought down Garret's first government, which had two incidental effects on our company. The first was that Fine Gael, in the person of the clever former businessman Peter Prendergast, rang Bunny to ask what retainer would be required to ensure the party had our exclusive services in the few weeks leading up to the general election. Bunny picked a sum out of the air and Prendergast agreed to it with such alacrity that Chief (as we all called Bunny) immediately felt he hadn't asked for enough. The next question discombobulated him even more. Would he run for Fine Gael in a named constituency? Bunny quickly said he was enormously flattered but no thank you. He was later asked to be a Fianna Fáil candidate and a Labour Party contender. The answer was the same, although I have no doubt he would love to have run for Fine Gael.

With the campaign under way, I was surprised to take a phone call on behalf of Bunny from Fine Gael one day which began with the caller asking if I recalled that my company had committed to work exclusively with their party until polling day. I got shirty, telling the caller that I recalled it pretty well and that we had met the conditions of that retainer punctiliously. The caller immediately acknowledged that, explaining they had another issue in mind. Like?

'If Fine Gael paid you, would you make a party political broadcast for the Labour Party?'
'Sorry?'

He explained that the Labour Party hadn't expected a general election so soon after the last one – who had? – and were short of cash to fight it. Since Fine Gael was in partnership with Labour and hoped to continue in partnership with them after the election, all going well, the party was prepared to provide the funding for us to do a party political for them. Fine Gael would have neither influence nor control over the content of the broadcast. That was totally up to Labour. Were we up for it? We were. I dealt with the Director of Elections for Labour, Ruairi Quinn, who was clear in his briefings and brisk in his judgement of the rushes. Some of the footage was wonderful. A dark tunnel with a stone staircase inside, right beside our Taney Road Railway Station offices struck me as perfect for a symbolic opening, for which I exploited my toddler son, who still resents being used for political purposes. It isn't that he doesn't like the Labour Party, but that he firmly believes using children in publicly consumed footage cuts across the privacy rights they are too young to understand or exercise. Mainly, though, I think he sulks over not getting paid. He didn't even get a cream bun, as he did when we used him in a Superquinn training video.

Whatever about Anton's mixed views, he was wonderful in the party political, climbing up the dark steps and emerging into glorious sunshine with the happiest smile as he personified Ireland's glorious future under a coalition government starring Labour. Some of the other footage was less wonderful. I filmed Michael D. Higgins and Michael O'Leary together and it was a nightmare trying to get the two of them into the same shot, so florid was the mutual loathing. When I made some negative comment about the two of them in comparison to the professionalism of Dick Spring, despite his being in agony from a back injury, Quinn smartly and unemotionally ticked me off. The party political was broadcast, highly praised and immediately forgotten, as are 99.9 per cent of party politicals, with the exception of Labour's 'Nessun Dorma' broadcast publicising Mary Robinson during her presidential campaign, directed by Eoghan Harris.

No party won a decisive majority in that election, but Fianna Fáil showed an amazing determination to be in government, although it wasn't until much later that we learned about Brian Lenihan Sr contacting President Patrick Hillery at Áras an Uachtaráin, in advance of the collapse of the coalition administration, to controversially try to persuade him to refuse to dissolve the Oireachtas and enable Haughey to enter the Taoiseach's office without a competition. Hillery refused.

But Haughey was getting there, by hook or by crook, and so deals had to be done. The deal-maker in this case was Tony Gregory, a working-class Northsider who had started his political career by joining the IRA and Sinn Féin, later fighting local authority and Oireachtas elections as an Independent. When Haughey came a-wooing, Gregory knew what he wanted and had the sense to have a witness to the negotiations (Michael Mullen of the Irish Transport and General

Workers' Union). Everything in what became known as the Gregory deal was written down and made public. Gregory's own impoverished and neglected constituency did well out of a deal worth a hundred million quid at the time. Garret, his focus on national objectives rather than placating a Northside TD, offered Gregory markedly less.

In the event, the quick collapse of the administration the Gregory deal helped to create meant that many of the promises therein were never fulfilled. It did, however, teach a pivotal lesson in negotiation to Independents who might choose to support an incoming minority or coalition government: do the deal with witnesses and get it in writing.

Gregory seems to have insisted that the photograph commemorating the deal be taken by national media on his turf. That shot showed Gregory on the bike he used to travel around his constituency with Charlie Haughey beside him, wearing a forced smile of abject gratitude.

4

Concentrating on Losing Money

*P*olitical communication was a low priority for the company in the early 1980s. We were too busy losing money. We missed no opportunity to make corporately costly mistakes, while expanding our staff numbers and our income, which two we mistakenly understood to mean that we were playing a blinder.

We were bang up to date in markets and technology, or so we thought, having bought a second-hand BBC outside broadcast unit which was physically impressive and actually useless, and that's not even mentioning the fact that we paid for it out of borrowings, whereas had we talked to the IDA, where Bunny had once been a director, most of the cost of a brand new one would have been met by the state.

The big trend at the time was corporate videos, and so we recklessly expanded the numbers of TV production staff. Not that we thought of ourselves as reckless. We were too busy congratulating ourselves on being ahead of the posse and surrounded by such talented creatives. We were making the overwhelming bulk of Ireland's promotional and training videos, and seeing our logo go up at the conclusion of a production was such a charge. Our end-of-year figures were fattened by the production unit's fees.

Because many of our training clients came back to us after their course to ask for public relations advice, we developed a PR unit, too, and recruited people for it. None of the director/shareholders – Bunny, Tom, Dominic McNamara and me – interrogated the decision as we would have when advising external clients, and so PR limped along, uncherished, as part of our offering. Because of surrender business, it washed its face, as did video production, but that was the height of it.

My godawful car crash in the mid-eighties was possibly the best thing that ever happened to our corporate bottom line. Virtually every bone in my body other than those in my right arm was broken, my teeth were smashed and my appearance changed for good. To this day, I cannot bear to watch myself on TV because my face doesn't work the way it should. (Other people may not be able to bear watching me on TV for other reasons.)

It wasn't great for Tom either. Our company might have been putting a lot of money through its books, but only at the cost of tiny salaries for its shareholders. None of us had ever related the word 'dividend' to ourselves as shareholders, which was just as well, because when you're losing money each and every year, dividends are not a possibility. To make ends meet, Tom took other jobs. One was as the first producer of RTÉ radio's *Morning Ireland*, where he articulated many of the principles that led to its defining success and its continuation to today. Today, when you read about work-from-homers doing three full-time jobs at the same time, their energy and commitment look impressive. However, they're sitting on their arses at home without a commute or the need to negotiate, face-to-face, with colleagues.

Tom's days were rather more demanding. He had to be in RTÉ Donnybrook before 5 a.m. to talk to the night editors and look at the news feeds from Reuters, Press International, Bloomberg and others. Writing links and directing researchers was followed by briefing the two presenters (often the gruff David Hanly, a wonderful writer who is still with us, and David Davin-Power, who is not). Then it was into the control room for pre-recordings followed by the live broadcast, after which came the de-brief and outline planning for the following day's offering.

When the *Morning Ireland* task was done, Tom would drive to the Old Railway Station in Dundrum to run courses or do consultations for the day. Editorship of the *Irish Medical Journal*, a weekly rival to John O'Connell's *Irish Medical Times*, came a little later in the eighties, requiring his presence in that office from about five o'clock on. Three jobs, one day.

Hugh McGowan, our bank manager, lived on faith and confusion. On the one hand, the company he had given us money to fund was doing an enormous amount of work for substantial fees while always failing to make a profit. One of its director-shareholders, Tom, was doing rightly, in financial terms, by varied and extensive work. I was half-working in the company while – courtesy of an invitation from publisher Catherine Rose – beginning to write books about communications, starting with *Write and Get Paid For It*.

Then my car collided head-on with another near Lucan. I came back to work within a month, using a wheelchair, but it became obvious that my long-term memory was goosed in a way that dictated my training work be limited. Course participants tend to be unhappy with a tutor who, having worked with them for years, suddenly cannot remember who they are or for whom they work.

Since normal work was not possible, I decided it would be good for me to learn more about corporate finances, so I asked our financial controller to take me through the books. It was one of the grimmer experiences of my career to find that we were doing so badly. A solid decade of losses stared back at me from the spreadsheet as the financial controller told me that while Bunny, Tom and I were very good at training, we were useless at running a business. She clarified: we might possibly be good at it if we ever concentrated on it, but we never did.

I asked her what we were missing. Profit, she said. Throughput means nothing. Income means nothing. Expansion means nothing. All that matters is profit, and that is not prioritised in this company. I didn't tell her – because she had probably worked it out by herself

– that I was a major contributor to this inattention, believing firmly that if we were doing rakes of stuff, we had to be a success. Not so, I now realised. Therefore? I asked. Therefore, she said briskly, the video production unit needs to close right now. I looked at the numbers of staff involved and instinctively shook my head before realising that options were there none. In advance of me talking to the directors, would she get our accountants to come up with redundancy offers that were generous – ideally generous enough to allow any of them who wanted to set up their own companies to do so and be sub-contracted by us? They did and we parted from some twenty people on good terms, continuing to work with several of them while watching others become serious content-makers long before that term was current.

We decided that the PR division could become more profitable and I took action to ensure that happened. But above all, I told Bunny and Tom, marketing had to be a priority. Meaning that the two of them had to make cold calls. Particularly Bunny, whose name would open any door. I gave each of them a list of individuals to cold call. One of Bunny's said yes, they could do with training their sales people. A two-day course was agreed. This all seemed very promising, until Bunny came to the office at the end of the first day and announced that he wouldn't be going back the second day, because he had told the high-tech company involved to fire its sales force because they didn't understand what they were selling, and, instead, to train their computer engineers to do strategic selling. I worried about this as an outcome, but forgot it while other clients responded to the cold calls. About six months later, the high-tech company involved came back to say they had done as recommended and it had rendered Ireland the only successful outpost of that company in that financial year. This, in turn, had attracted the attention of their headquarters, which had decided to implement the new model and to hire the Irish communications consultancy to do the training required.

Bunny and Tom, together with a wonderful Scottish executive named Ian Dand, developed a suite of training courses with supporting materials scripted by me, and set off across Europe, initially, to provide the training. That training was subsequently extended to Canada and the USA, where a computer genius named Bill Fitzgerald (dubbed 'The Marine' by Tom because Bill fitted Tom's picture of what a Marine should look like, although he'd never actually been *semper fi*) adopted us and, when he moved on from his first company, introduced us to subsequent employers.

What had looked like dire news directly after my car crash turned out to be a breakthrough and, although we continued to do political work, including with British and American politicians, and happily continued to comment whenever asked about political communication, it became even less important to us, despite being the first association many people made when our name was mentioned.

We could not but be aware that women were becoming more interested in political careers. It is instructive to look at the Houses of the Oireachtas infographic about the percentage of women and men elected to the Dáil from 1918 to 2018. The first one, showing 1918, has a single female TD. The woman who appears as a little red Lego figure was Constance Markievicz. That was the first Dáil. The second Dáil saw Markievicz joined by five other women. Start of a pattern? Nuh uh. Skip to 1981 and only eleven little red figures appear in a block of blue shapes representing lads. Move to 2011 and the red figures almost double, but are still in the minority by quite a distance.

That said, the selection process was gradually shifting. Habits change slowly, though, and the habit for nigh on three-quarters of a century was for women to become TDs through a sympathy vote because of the death of a father, a husband or sometimes a brother. Women running in their own right, not so much. While feminism, starting in Ireland at the beginning of the seventies as 'women's liberation', had an impact on a country where, at the time, marital rape was not a crime, where a woman had to present her husband's signature when seeking a library card, and where the civil service forcibly retired a female employee when she married, the number of female TDs increased so slowly that in 2016 there were thirty-five, or 22 per cent of the total.

When women who were not widows or daughters of TDs came to us to talk about their prospects of election, we got into the habit of asking an early question to test the waters.

'How ambitious are you?' we would ask, knowing that if we asked that question of an aspirant male TD, he was likely to tell us he was fairly ambitious and would like in a few years to be a minister. Women, asked the same question, would become uncomfortable and tell us they were unwilling to describe themselves as ambitious. Why? We never got a good answer but gradually came to apprehend what that answer might be. A woman declaring herself to be ambitious, whether in politics or in business, rendered herself instantly rejectable. Ambition was not regarded as a pleasing trait in a woman, and the sad part is that this is still the case. Despite generations of contenders on programmes like *The Apprentice* announcing themselves to be so ambitious they wanted the presenter's job the day after tomorrow, women still find themselves disliked if they claim to be ambitious. It supposedly makes them less 'relatable'. Although perhaps 'supposedly' is unfair. Whenever a woman publicly fails, one of the traits identified about her is that she was 'very ambitious'. Nobody ever disapprovingly described Michael O'Leary of Ryanair as 'very ambitious'. He wouldn't be where he is if he wasn't, and he doesn't give a sugar if you don't like it.

Public dislike of ambition on the part of women was nothing, as an obstacle to entering politics, when compared with the male hierarchy. The cumann or local organisation was overwhelmingly male and the men who ran it liked it fine that way. So the first thing we had to do, when assessing a woman's chances of making it into the Dáil, was to amputate her fear of being seen as ambitious. She had to know how far she was prepared to go and she had to come to terms with the prospect of being disliked and plotted against.

It was at that point that we lost many women; they simply couldn't face either of those possibilities. Some women who stayed were never going to make it, though, because they would plaintively point out to me that this was not the way it should be. Persuading them that 'should' had to be banned from their lexicon often took time. It's tough to perceive your chosen profession as being about resilience, ambition, drive and numbers when idealism runs through you and leads to you talking about the situation that 'should' obtain.

Although the 'frequently asked questions' system emerged from NASA in the early 1980s, any of the senior consultants in our company could tell you slightly before then what questions were most frequently asked by women who were thinking about a political career or already locally embedded in their party. Those questions always started with appearance. Should they lose weight? Since I was a good thirty kilos overweight during most of this period, they felt less self-conscious asking me the question than if I had been model-thin.

We never suggested to any politician, male or female, that they lose weight, but when asked, we had to tell women in particular that in our research and elsewhere, it was apparent that the first thing people, no matter their gender, registered about a woman on TV was if she was overweight, and they noticed it negatively, making an instantaneous judgement against her. To sit in a pub when Gay Byrne's *Late Late Show* was being broadcast was to be educated in just how many denigratory terms this country has for female avoirdupois. Overweight men never seemed to provoke such comments. Like, yer man might be on the big side, but what of it? If a woman was being discussed, substantive questions surfaced in the pub. Like 'Who ate all the pies?' And although people have become a little more cautious in articulating this prejudice, it's only a little.

After the weight question came the wardrobe question: what should they wear? Many of the women we met, in those early days, had favourite dresses they would love to have worn on TV and were dismayed when we told them No Sequins, No Satin, No Cleavage. No sequins because they breach a fundamental rule to be obeyed by any serious woman on TV: don't wear anything that's louder than you are. Sequins break that rule, as does satin, as do enormous active hoop earrings and necklaces spelling out the names of your grandchildren. No Cleavage came as a surprise to many of our early visitors, although they quickly got the hang of it when told that it might make them appear more attractive and frankly more sexy, but did they want a male TV watcher to spend a programme speculating about his chances with you, rather than listening to your argument? Similarly, did they want a female TV viewer to go 'Jesus, would you look at your one! Where does she think she's going in that?'

Whenever we did recordings with women in our studios, even though in the early days those women were few and far between and tended to come from business, journalism or education rather than from politics, we had observed a common factor it behoved us to warn political women about: the low neckline. Even if the neckline finished short of potential cleavage, a low neckline still held dangers, because women under stress tend to blush, and when they blush, they blush from below breast level right up to the face. They blush blotchily, too, which can be revealed by a low neckline. Ergo, since appearing on TV is inevitably a pretty stressful experience, a dress or top with a high neckline may be advisable.

Bitter experience, direct or indirect, gave rise to much of the advice we gave and still give to female political candidates. One *Prime Time* TV programme a few years ago featured several female politicians, three of them wearing the same red jacket. They could have been Butlin's Redcoats in the old days, and, having watched the programme, we invariably told female politicians to bring an alternative jacket with them to avoid a recurrence.

Men have it easier when it comes to TV. Avoiding ties with ambiguous pictures on them and socks, likewise, makes common sense. Yes, we remember Leo Varadkar and Justin Trudeau getting competitive with decorative socks. We do remember that. We shouldn't and we don't want to. Of course, what you wear on TV is peripheral to your central purpose. It matters only to the extent that it assists or detracts from your achievement of that purpose. In which context, it is worth remembering the origin of air crew uniforms. In the early days of passenger aviation, newcomers to flying were understandably terrified of the whole adventure. (These days, they're more scared of disruptive drunk fellow-passengers.) Someone copped on that the air crew needed to look like they were competently in charge, and how better to convey that understanding than by dressing them as if they were army officers? It worked, and to this day the cabin crew of major airlines are immediately identifiable as they arrive at the departure gate.

The lesson to be drawn from that is that a tailored jacket is still useful in its implication of authority. Contrast colours are also useful. You may be more comfortable in grey fleece casuals, but you're entering people's homes. Show them the respect you would show them if you were their guest. Dressing up a little won't either kill you or falsify you.

The wider question few female politicians ask, although many of them would like to, is how important being pretty is when it comes to getting votes. The sad answer is that it's become more important, not less, in recent years. Women don't obsessively edit and filter their photographs on Instagram without good reason, and the good reason is that appearance matters more in recent times. The old preference in newspaper pictures for models and other glamour girls has transferred – on steroids – to social media. Top influencers are not regnant because they work hard. Most of them have achieved their influencer niche because they're good-looking. Try flogging jeans online without looking spectacular in them, and you're going nowhere, no matter how beautifully curated your online platform.

That wasn't what was envisaged when feminism took off in the 1970s. Many of the instructive influencers of the time truly hated what Betty Friedan called 'the feminine mystique', starring the wasp-waisted, perky-boobed little wives of the ads of the 1950s and 1960s, pictured in full-skirted delight at the very prospect of wielding a vacuum cleaner on whatever dust might have settled overnight in their pristine homes. The women driving feminism in the latter half of the twentieth century condemned any emphasis on appearance and rejected the idea that you had to be good-looking to succeed. But here's the thing. Rejecting an idea doesn't mean the idea goes off into a corner where it curls up and dies. Feminism has always fallen at this fence, convinced that something so obvious will become operational truth immediately after it has been identified. It didn't and doesn't.

Instead of writing columns condemning the moral and employment judgements made against overweight or unattractive women (as I did in the 1980s), we should, of course, have positioned this as a human rights issue and ensured that auditions and job interviews were 'blind', so that the appearance of the actor or job applicant could not influence the interviewers or producers. (This has proven remarkably effective when auditioning instrumentalists for orchestras.)

Over time, the looks issue boiled down to eye-rolling when someone compliments a little girl on how attractive she is or tells a colleague or friend that they look gorgeous. It's a particularly unproductive form of censorship based on reversing the 'if you see it, you can be it' theory. The reverse theory is that if you don't hear it said, it can't be real. Which, combined with the body positivity movement and #MeToo, should mean that women can be successful without reference to their appearance.

Who are we kidding? Women who don't look good can be successful. Of course they can – as long as they work twice as hard as everybody else and have twice as many brain cells. Bosses maintain that looks never influence their choices at all, but evidence has repeatedly emerged identifying a striking link between career success and being physically attractive. It's even got its own title: the Pretty Privilege.

In January 2025, for example, researchers from the Institute for Operations Research and the Management Sciences in Baltimore, Maryland analysed the careers of more than 40,000 graduates who had earned MBAs. They found the Pretty Privilege in play, big-time, at all stages in the careers of the 40,000 people. The professor who led the study didn't put a tooth in it, claiming that 'Appearance shapes not just the start of a career, but its trajectory over decades. These findings reveal a persistent and compounding effect of beauty in professional settings.'

In other words, not only were the more attractive jobseekers more likely to get the jobs they wanted, they were also paid more than 10 per cent more than colleagues who didn't compete in the looks department and were more likely to be promoted. Game, set and match to the lookers. Doesn't seem like the enlightened frowning at eejits who tell first holy communicants that they look like princesses is having much effect, does it?

I am not saying we shouldn't dial down on the gratuitous complimenting of women, young and old, on their appearance. Of course we should. What I am saying is that we shouldn't fool ourselves that such well-meaning semi-censorship achieves anything significant. Good-looking people have always been favoured by life, although few so floridly as current examples, like, for instance, Kim Kardashian. Right now, while we may – rightly – control our desire to tell children how pretty they are, the fact is that the underlying reality still matters. The better-looking you are, the bigger your pay slip. The taller you are, in America, the more likely you are to win a presidential election. The more gorgeous you are, the more likely the jury is to find you innocent.

One résumé-building firm, StandOut CV, says conventionally attractive employees can earn markedly more than their average-looking peers. This piece of research may not be deep science, but it's relevant all the same. 'We asked respondents to rate how conventionally attractive they are and compared this to how successful they are, to find out how far looks (or body confidence) really does impact your career', researchers from the company say. 'Not only are attractive people treated preferentially, but those deemed less attractive are actively disfavored.'

We cannot be shocked by this when the US president repeatedly makes reference to the appearance of women and employs women who look alike in their slender, long-haired pulchritude. We should not behave as if we're helpless in the face of social media persuading pre-teenage children that they need moisturiser and have to lose weight to fit into the model of what is acceptable.

The 1950s model of the acceptable woman was limited and limiting. But probably not as limited and limiting as the current one. It's something that aspirant female politicians need to be aware of and move past. One beautiful TD once sent me a query as to why her photograph was appearing in stories to which she had no or only the most tenuous connection. I told her to get a grip, that she knew bloody well her looks were impelling the picture selection. Her philosophical response was, 'Having started out "awkward" and turned into "pretty" I am aware of how the world treats each. And even now I have to spend a fortune to maintain it and can't afford to look tired, because the pictures last for ever.'

5

Crossing Colonel Gaddafi's Rug

John O'Connell understood media as an insider, having founded and edited the phenomenally successful *Irish Medical Times*. He started to nag Haughey about Fianna Fáil's rotten media image in the wake of outbreaks of GUBU, and to talk to me about the same problem.

'He has to come here to you,' Dr John kept telling me.

'Two chances of that ever happening, John,' was the usual reply.

'If he asked you to go out to Kinsealy, would you?'

'Sure. But he won't'.

One Saturday morning, John rang about 9 a.m.

'Terry. Do you remember you said you'd go to Kinsealy if Mr Haughey asked you to?'

'Yes?'

'Well, he's asked me to ask you.'

'Oh. When?'

'Now. I'll pick you up in half an hour.'

An hour later, I was making my way, with difficulty – still on crutches after the car crash – across the hall carpet (gift of Colonel Gaddafi) in the beautiful Gandon-designed home of the Haugheys, headed for Mr Haughey's small study. Tea was served in paper-thin china cups. Haughey sat behind a mahogany desk, Dr John and I in chairs on the other side of it. Haughey invited me to discuss the recent media appearances of members of his front bench. As I talked, he began to twirl the big leather chair on which he sat sideways, slowly, then more sideways, until he was in profile, facing away from me. I faltered.

'You're depressing me,' he growled.

'Well, look at it this way, Mr Haughey, at least you're getting it for free,' I said.

At this point Dr John rose to his feet and delivered an impassioned statement on the importance of electronic media (although he didn't use that phrase), expatiating on recent overseas examples of politicians felled because they would not pay attention to, or learn the rules of, radio and television. Haughey watched him in silence, his chin tucked into his neck, his small pale hands fiddling with items on the desk. To avert my gaze from the hands, I looked at the floor, to see that Dr John was wearing mismatched shoes, no doubt the product of his belief in the importance of the session and his high level of tension about it. From where he sat I doubted that CJ could see John's shoes.

When John had finished his rant, Haughey looked at him, then rose, and without a word, led us to the front door. He thanked us for our time and off we went. I told John I was sorry I'd wrecked his chances of getting Fianna Fáil camera-friendly, but that if Haughey didn't want to be told the truth about his wafflers, we weren't a great place to start. John grinned, which was disconcerting, and knowingly told me he'd be back to me. He was. Two days later, a pilot course for frontbenchers was booked in.

In the event, the course had to be postponed because of a three-line whip in Leinster House. On the day when it was supposed to happen, however, one evening newspaper ran a column by John Feeney (who later died in a small plane crash on his way back from France along with other journalists bringing home the new season Beaujolais). This column announced that Fianna Fáil was sending its top bods up to us to be taught to smile and say, 'I'm glad you asked me that question.'

(Just for the record, that, like smiling at the end of a sentence, is one of the idiot pieces of advice we have never, ever given to any politician. Or any other client, for that matter.) In this instance, we could only seethe and shrug.

In the middle of a crowded open office the following day, all conversation halted when Tom, immersed in a phone call, raised his voice, just a little, to say fiercely, 'Just one minute, Mr Haughey. I'll not take that from you or from any man.' Everyone froze. Apparently, Haughey, telephoning to re-book the course, had barked a stinger: 'And could we have confidentiality this time?' It was at that point that Tom barked right back, refusing to accept the accusation. Tom told him he could look to his own people for the source of the newspaper leak because our company did not leak. Ever. Haughey asked why he should believe that.

'Very simple,' Tom told him. 'Three of your frontbenchers, despite your declaring a fatwa on this company, come regularly to us for media coaching. You don't know who they are, and you'll never know – from us.'

Haughey grumbled his parting and a week or so later half a dozen frontbenchers duly arrived to the Old Railway Station, where we were based at the time. They included Máire Geoghegan-Quinn, Michael Noonan (the Fianna Fáil version, immediately dubbed by Bunny 'the Minister for Green Wellies'), Charlie McCreevy and Pádraig Flynn. Máire Geoghegan-Quinn might have been the most impressive woman I had ever met. Or have ever met since. Tall, with long straight jet-black hair and impeccably manicured hands, she had an air of distance I was later to find out was generated by shyness. She was also one of the few present who was unintimidated by Pádraig Flynn, who, from the outset, acted as a sniper on his colleagues, jeering at them with enough force to visibly reduce their desire to engage in any conversation. This was particularly noticeable around the big circular table in Bunny's office at lunch on the first of the two days of the course. As I remember it, Michael Noonan said something. Flynn said something snide. Tom, sitting beside me, leaped to his feet, leaned across the table, grasped Flynn by the lapels of his jacket and said, 'Shut up, you.'

We all sat in paralysed silence.

'We don't tolerate verbal terrorism here,' Tom told him. 'So you have a choice. Either you stay silent, except when physically recording an exercise, or you leave now. Which is it?'

Flynn stared at him.

'Silence gives consent', Tom said, 'so I am assuming you agree to our conditions.'

He sat down and, as if nothing had happened, started to talk to the frontbencher sitting beside him. Bunny and I took our cue from him and began to talk to our table mates. Flynn sat and ate his lunch without a word. After lunch, I led half the group (including Flynn) into the studio, where I was effecting the video recording of speeches being made by each of them. By that stage I had realised that I could not handle assessments. The car crash had delivered just enough brain damage to ruin my short-term memory and give me unexpected blackouts. This was to improve – somewhat – over time, but it limited what I could do in the months directly after the accident. Each of the six in my group recorded their talks. Tom was recording the other six in Bunny's office and Bunny was having a long slow smoke of his pipe in the car park to recover from the lunchtime fracas.

Pádraig Flynn was second last in the recording order and he delivered a speech that properly belonged to a man on the back of a lorry: a bellowed disconnected barrage of assertions about Fianna Fáil. I changed the tape and made no comment. The last participant did his speech and I gathered five cassettes together and handed them to Geoghegan-Quinn.

'Tom will be waiting for you in Bunny's office. You know how to get to it? Good. Deputy Flynn, perhaps you'd wait here for just a minute?'

The others headed off. I shoved the videocassette into the player and turned to Flynn.

'Mr Flynn, I don't know anything about you. But you have someone who's close to you. Wife. Lover. Someone from whom you have no secrets. Give me a first name?'

'Dorothy.'

'Okay.' I took away his notes. 'Could you do your talk only to Dorothy? Nobody else. Anytime I hear you saying something I don't believe you'd say to her, I'll stop the tape. Five, four, three, two – go.'

He didn't start immediately. But then he began to talk. Talk, not bellow. Talk with a gentleness and a desire to be interesting that changed the performance completely. When he was done, I thanked him, took the cassette and was trying to get the wheelchair into the corridor through the awkward double doors of the studio when he took the handles, tilted it back as only people used to wheeling wheelchairs know how to do, and propelled me in front of him to Bunny's office, where he moved away and sat down among the others, who were coming to the end of a playback. Tom acknowledged us both with a nod but no more than that. When he was ready to move on, I handed him the videocassette.

'Two versions of the same talk, one after another,' I muttered. Up to him to do what he could with the extra recording.

'Let's just play the two in their totality, and comment then,' Tom said, and pushed the button so the group – including the six who had recorded elsewhere – got the full brunt of untrammelled Flynn in rabble-rouser mode. Most of the participants watched the screen, too terrified of Flynn even to snigger. Geoghegan-Quinn, who was seated out of his line of sight, gave me an outrageous wink in the middle of that first rendition. Then the screen went to black, brightening again after five seconds. None of them had seen this second recording, and as they watched it they sneaked occasional glances at Flynn, who looked neither right nor left. The quality of the silence changed as the black and white figure on screen thought aloud, because that was what he was doing. At the end, after a pause, someone started to clap and they all joined in.

'Don't really need to assess this at the usual length,' Tom said. 'The first recording is a waste of time. The speaker is talking to himself. The second is authentic good communication and seems to be directed to a real listener. That's how to do it.'

Pádraig Flynn stood up and told Tom that he hadn't come to us to be verbally or physically abused. A flicker of a smile passed over Tom's face at the notion that being grabbed around the lapels by a much smaller man was physical abuse. But, Flynn went on, both had occurred anyway and he had to say they might be the best things that had ever happened to him. He had learned an enormous amount about himself and about communication and, if we were willing, would be our friend for life. We digested this in silence.

'And Dorothy is my *wife*,' he told me crossly.

The following day, Mr Flynn said little, but what he said was pertinent, helpful and showed considerable understanding of the communications principles adduced the previous day. At the end of the session, each group was asked to fill in their 'smile sheets' – the forms on which they rated how good or bad the training delivered to them had been. I gathered them up and the two groups came together in Bunny's office to have glasses of wine, over which Geoghegan-Quinn, McCreevy and Flynn giving each other stick was pure comedy.

The expectation, before the course, was that as Haughey's self-proclaimed gauleiter, the big Mayo man would go straight out to Kinsealy and tell the boss to reinstate his ban on Fianna Fáil members coming to us. Flynn did go out to Kinsealy, but what he told the boss was to (a) send all TDs on the course and (b) undergo media training with us himself.

The first happened immediately, with all participants told that Haughey had demanded a brief report from Tom Savage on each of them. Haughey didn't want them told about this report, but Tom wasn't going to be set up as some kind of spy, so he informed them. For the most part, he found instincts, skills or effort worth mentioning to CJ in the paragraph-long reports, smiling to himself as he typed, knowing bloody well that what Haughey wanted was the most waspish negativity Tom could muster. The only time he came near either was when, after trying desperately to find something positive to say about one TD, he ended up typing 'This man wears good suits well.' Inevitably, this was the reference out of more than a hundred that CJ referred to with most relish, despite the fact that the suit-wearer was one of his most faithful consiglieri, who functioned as eyes and ears on the ground within the party for the leader and who was always welcome in the inner sanctum.

Charlie Haughey was like someone with a loose tooth – he couldn't keep his tongue away from the pleasure of probing the weakness. And he deliberately surrounded himself with weakness. In *The Spy and the Traitor*, Ben Macintyre tells how Pavel Sudoplatov, one of Stalin's spymasters, had this advice for his officers seeking to recruit spies in Western countries:

> Search for people who are hurt by fate or nature – the ugly, those suffering from an inferiority complex, craving power and influence but defeated by unfavourable circumstances ... In co-operation with us, all these find a peculiar compensation. The sense of belonging to an influential and powerful organisation will give them a feeling of superiority over the handsome and prosperous people around them.

Sudoplatov might have been explaining Haughey's preference for the weak or flawed over the able and virtuous. For one of life's people 'defeated by unfavourable circumstances,' even a single encounter with Mr Haughey was close to transubstantiation. Favoured by even fleeting attention from him, they would subsequently search out any tiny snippets of information – ideally about the treachery of others – that could be brought to him as offerings to an Aztec god's altar. He could and did treat them with contempt in front of others, use them as intellectual punchbags to prove to another layer of friends how clever he and that upper layer were, but, like beaten dogs, they would always come back to their owner, and Mr Haughey truly owned them. His very cruelty showed them they registered with him and mattered to him, even if negatively. And then, when he included them in a snide joke, for them it was akin to being assumed back into heaven.

His friendship with, and political adoption of, Dr John O'Connell was part of that. He needed John because John was rich and connected with even richer men. But, on top of that, Charles Haughey could not have missed John's aching need for a hero, and, unlikely as it might seem, for perhaps two years, Haughey stepped into that role for John. He was the man who was going to solve the problems of the North, he was the man who was going to drag Fianna Fáil back into respectability. Once John fell out of love with Labour, he was a political loose boot, looking for a foot to wear him. He could keep a secret, too, and so at the time nobody other than me knew about his friendship with Haughey. That secrecy, of course, suited Mr Haughey down to the ground. This was a leader who never saw a conspiracy he didn't want to lead.

John was also amazingly persuasive. His capacity to convince by persistence was unequalled. Once his teeth were sunk in your leg, nothing would pry them loose. He would tackle you with gifts, once unsuccessfully trying to give my husband a motorised golf cart, at a time when nothing like it had ever been seen on an Irish golf course, But he would also deploy charm, argument, rage and pathos. Most people eventually gave in. As Haughey did. The Fianna Fáil leader came for his first media training session late one evening, accompanied by Dr John, who was grinning like a child at having brought the man around.

We had the studio beautifully set up, cyclorama in smooth backdrop, fully lit for a formal half-hour interview with him. Bunny was due to do the interview, but halfway through the afternoon, he got the bends about it. Even though we were not retained by Fine Gael, who had demanded and paid for exclusive service only coming up to one particular general election, Bunny felt a loyalty to Garret that made him uncomfortable at the prospect of training Haughey. Tom interrogated Bunny, asking him where we differed from lawyers and doctors in our obligation to provide professional services to people with whom we disagreed, and that made it worse. Of course we didn't have the right to make moral judgements about those whose personal values or morals we despised, Bunny agreed. Of course, if we were not actually being asked to help someone articulate something evil, we would be getting way above ourselves and also reducing our market to a tiny elite if we refused to coach people we didn't like, approve of or trust. Of course driving instructors didn't refuse to teach people of one particular political persuasion. Of course dentists didn't refuse the obligation to yank a bad tooth if that bad tooth occupied a space within the head of a political dud. But because Bunny was so visibly distressed Tom told him to go home, that I would do the interview, and after a token protest, he got into the Jag and drove to Sutton.

I hadn't told Dr John who would be doing the interview, so when Mr Haughey was led into a studio and found one of the matching black leather thrones occupied by me, he seemed to assume that this was as planned. I did a kitchen-sink interview: everything got thrown, including Colonel Gaddafi's carpet and Terry Keane. (It should be remembered that this was at least fifty years ago, when the Keane love affair was widely rumoured, but not known for sure, even to Seán, the son who later succeeded Haughey in his constituency.)

At the end of the interview, Mr Haughey was good and mad. After I thanked him, the cameras continued to record because that was how I had briefed the camera operators, and so they captured him leaning across, grasping me by the knee and telling me I was a rude bitch. It was said half-furiously, half-appreciatively.

The tape was rewound, a pot of weak tea brought, and assessment begun. Haughey was initially defensive, resentfully – and wrongly – predicting what criticisms I would make. Once he copped on that assessment wasn't the same as criticism, he became fascinated by it, curious about what distinguished the written from the spoken word and intrigued by the need to be singular and specific, rather than general and conceptual. We probably got only seven minutes into the recording, because even when you interview somebody for forty minutes, as I had in this case, everything you need is to be found in the first minutes. The reason we would play a recording from start to finish is because the density of concentration on the first minute or two is beyond most people, although it wasn't beyond Haughey. He questioned everything, making occasional notes. He was engaged, insightful, observant and funny, using his own videotape as a case study through which to explore the dynamic of TV interviews generally.

And he kept revising. Reminding himself that conceptual language wouldn't work on TV, which was hard for him to move into performance because he thought and spoke exclusively in conceptual language. But he grasped that forcing viewers to imagine something by describing it to them helped it into their short-term memory and then into long-term memory. It was one of the most engrossing times I've ever had with any kind of participant on a training course.

Inevitably, a good mind presented with tangible evidence in such a situation has to either dig in, double down or move. Haughey moved, reluctantly but not slowly, from a view of TV interviewers as enemies motivated by spite, personal ambition and 'Sticky' (Workers' Party) affiliation to a view of them as seeking to provide something vitally interesting and memorable for their viewers; a position which allows an interviewee to contribute positively, rather than go on the run, verbally. Time passed without us noticing, until Tom came in.

'Mr Haughey', he said, 'you may be willing to continue and Tess may be willing to continue with you. But there's a point at which learning stops and that point happened about a half an hour ago.'

Haughey asked me if I would look at the rest of it and send my notes, along with the tape, to Kinsealy. I nodded and off he went, in high good humour. Dr John, who had maintained a strangled silence throughout, was on cloud nine.

At seven o'clock the following morning, I was on my own in the office, Tom having dropped me off on his way to *Morning Ireland*, when the office phone rang. The caller was Mr Haughey. He wanted to say thank you for a most valuable session and to go over some of the points arising. In the middle of the conversation, he said he had been advised to have eyelid surgery. He said it, didn't state where the advice had originated and left it for me to address. I thought about him and his hooded eyes, and the immediate visual comparison between him the Fine Gael or Labour Party members with whom he might share a studio.

'If you have that surgery, it's going to make a difference –'

'For the better?'

'Oh, yes. But. People are going to talk about it. Media will ask about it and write and talk about it. Your eyelids will be the equivalent of Maggie Thatcher's lowered voice. It's you who'll decide whether the gain outweighs the losses.'

He barked something to the effect that he had no interest in image management and that he now knew that what he had to do was be interesting on television. It was the start of a pattern. Mr Haughey would ask for help – it might be in preparation for a TV or radio programme or a print interview. He was rare in his understanding that print interviewers needed as much valuable material presented to them as did broadcasters. He would rehearse, watch the playback, make notes of some of the assessment points made to him, and then do the programme. Invariably, he would telephone first thing the following morning to thank me and discuss – with ruthless self-assessment – precisely what he had managed to achieve and where he had failed. Not only was he generous – always recalling the detail of the remembered advice and how it had worked – but he took responsibility when things didn't work. That happened once in a leaders' debate, and once in an ard fheis.

The leaders' debate was with Dr FitzGerald. Haughey was hyper-aware that the early moments of any TV appearance were dominated by viewer reaction to the participants' appearance, and he was in no doubt that Garret the Good presented a scattered, absent-minded professor appearance rooted in good temper, whereas Haughey, not least because of the heavily hooded slate-coloured eyes, gave an impression of menace. Few people who didn't already like him related warmly to him as a result of a TV appearance.

In the dry run for the leaders' debate, Haughey was stunningly impressive in his grasp of every aspect of government policy, which wasn't a great surprise, since it was widely believed that he didn't trust any of his ministers to do the job without daily interventions from him, so he was necessarily up to speed in each department's doings. However, the recording showed him to be so impatient that he wasn't waiting for the end of questions. I told him that if he didn't listen – and listen analytically – he was going to come unstuck.

'If you answer a question that hasn't been asked, you're going to look like you're evading the question that *has* been asked,' I said.

He went down to RTÉ and I went home to watch the programme. Halfway through, Dr FitzGerald found a document in one of his pockets (his difficulty locating the bit of paper was classic Garret, great television and visibly irritating to Haughey) and made an accusation. Confusion ensued, with Haughey snapping at the wrong end of the stick. Furious, I stopped watching and went to bed. About an hour later, the phone rang and after a few minutes, my husband appeared at the bedroom door.

'That was Mr Haughey,' he said. 'He said to tell you he's sorry. That you'd warned him about not listening. And to thank you for your help.'

The second time he could – indeed, should – have blamed the helper was when I rewrote an ard fheis speech for him. Dr Martin Mansergh wrote the bulk of this and, indeed, all of Haughey's speeches, but gracefully submitted his prose to be translated into language more amenable to broadcast requirements. I shortened sentences, crafted emotional 'builds' and cut away more than a third of the original. The deletions created a small war among the advisers who came to watch Haughey rehearsing the autocued script. That bit about China had to be put back in. Bord na Móna couldn't be left out. The grassroots would want to hear the section that had been removed from page six. Haughey listened silently to all the comments and then nodded at me: speak.

'If you give yourself the space to deliver it well, you're guaranteed nine points of applause,' I said. 'Adding the time for that applause to the length of what you've just delivered will simply make the speech ten minutes too long.'

He made one small gesture and that was the end of it: the cuts stayed cut. The only problem was that I had underestimated the impact of the speech. It got thirteen, not nine, sustained natural bouts of applause, which ran it into the RTÉ news bulletin. Or would have, if RTÉ hadn't cut it off just as he was reaching the peroration. At home, I watched, with a sinking heart, the *Nine O'Clock News* graphics swimming across the screen. Fianna Fáil would be livid. (They were.) They would attack RTÉ. (They did.) They would also, and rightly, blame me. (Not so much, mainly because, since most of them did not know that Haughey prepared with me, they didn't make the correct blame-laying connection. P.J. Mara filled in that gap.)

Fifteen minutes into the news bulletin, our home phone rang. Tom indicated that he would take it if I wished, but I braced myself and took the call from Haughey. I apologised immediately. He dismissed any need for apology, said he was proud of the speech and had wanted to ring me quickly to thank me for my work on it. I put the phone down, weak with relief, knowing that the entire Fianna Fáil party in a full-blown rage would be easier to cope with than its leader in a similar state, and, anyway, once the word went out that Haughey was not furious, all would be well. Except, of course, for RTÉ, but Fianna Fáil fighting with RTÉ after a Haughey appearances of any kind was standard.

As time went on, our relationship with Haughey divided along clear lines. If he wanted to be prepped for a TV programme or helped with a speech, I was called. If he wanted to discuss policy or simply have an amusing chat over a cup of tea, Tom was chosen. Partly because he liked the way Tom analysed issues; partly because he knew Tom wasn't afraid of him. Charlie Haughey surrounded himself with people who were afraid of him, but loved the company of those who were not. That included politicians like Máire Geoghegan-Quinn and Fianna Fáil staff like Fionnuala O'Kelly, who headed his press office. But above all, it encompassed civil servants and external advisers who stood up to him because they knew their stuff and weren't intimidated by him. Hence he liked Tom. I was a coward, more comfortable dealing with the man in letters characterised by what Gaybo called my 'mannered subservience'. I preferred letters because of the ambivalence caused by my enjoying every training contact with him while at the same time regarding him as a fraud. Not a financial fraud: because finance and figures were not a strong point with me, I never understood any of the accusations made against him about whence his wealth had come.

The fraudulence I saw was his pretence of being a cultured man. His tax concession to artists was a clever and welcome move, but the fact is that his own understanding of the arts was thin. He had no particular liking for the theatre or for opera, and whenever he used a quotation, it came from the most obvious Leaving Cert set texts, right down to his claim, in his final speech, to have done the state some service. Nor – to be fair – did he ever seek to improve speeches by inserted quotations with which he was not familiar, although if they appeared in orations crafted by civil servants, he tended to leave them in place. This worked better than Paddy Duffy's approach to Bertie Ahern, the leader he served. Paddy was a classics scholar whose speeches for Bertie invariably contained references to or quotations from Ovid, Virgil or Seneca, although it was attributing quotations to classicists with more complicated names like Aeschylus and Sophocles that tended to make the Taoiseach fumble. Paddy Duffy never came to terms with the reality that Bertie's frame of reference did not include these writers. He kept implanting them, and constant misfiring deterred him not at all.

When it came to painting and sculpture, Homan Potterton, the director of the National Gallery, once told RTÉ's Seán O'Rourke that CJ 'didn't know a Titian from a turnip'. The paintings in his own home were nondescript and mutually unrelated. The cultivated country squire persona he confected for himself was accepted by Fianna Fáil backwoodsmen whose own grasp of the arts was loose, and by those who needed to go along with it for career reasons or were too scared to call him on it. He had an unequalled facility for terrifying and demeaning those who knew more about a subject than he did, to such an extent that Homan Potterton remembered his only visit to Abbeville as so fraught with anxiety as to render him amnesiac thereafter: he could not remember one single word exchanged between them in the course of a fairly lengthy visit.

Although he was always courteous to me, I was not thrilled when someone in the office one morning announced that Mr Haughey was on the phone, looking for Tom on a day when Tom was in Athens, training Greek electronics engineers in how to deal with customers. My heart did a bungee jump. Forget that cliché about hearts going into boots. Mine visited my extremities, then bounced back and hit my larynx. Not that Haughey was ever unpleasant to any of us. It was just that if he was ringing at 10 a.m., and looking for Tom Savage, then he had a problem unlikely to be solvable by me, and he would not be happy at Tom's unavailability.

I figured the problem had to do with the Progressive Democrats. The new party, led by Des O'Malley, was only a few weeks old at that point. But for a tiny newborn, it was creating one hell of a stir – mainly by inspired timing. A high-profile defection from a major political party would occupy the national attention for one week. Then there would be a lull, during which that party would convince itself that the departure wasn't a loss but a gain. At the same time, the media and the public would wonder if that was the end of it.

It never was. Just as the national pulse returned to normal, a press conference or photo call or mass meeting would be announced, and a high profiler from another big party would join the PDs. Even if you had no interest in politics, you were reached by the dramatic tension, and if you did have an interest in politics, you got sucked into the latest conspiracy theory. Around this time, it was believed that Charlie McCreevy or Séamus Brennan was definitely going to be the next mover from Fianna Fáil. When McCreevy and Brennan stayed glued to their FF seats, the explanation was that their tenure was temporary and that they would be departing in a matter of weeks. Theories abounded, and the PDs deployed what Mary Harney later defined as their great strength; in media terms, they punched way above their weight.

The morning Haughey telephoned our office looking for Tom, it was therefore probable that his problem related to this ongoing storm. It did. In a tense mutter, he told me that Bobby Molloy would be walking from Fianna Fáil within hours, his defection neatly timed to ensure that Haughey would be doorstepped at the entrance to the Burlington Hotel that evening, where he was guest of honour at an event, by a phalanx of journalists wanting to get his reaction to the latest runner from the ranks. Accordingly, what Haughey had wanted from Tom Savage was advice on whether he should simply walk past the media or say something to them, and if he was going to say something, what he should say.

'What's your own instinct about what you should say?'

I asked the question partly because only a half-witted consultant leaps into the breach, offering advice that's going to run counter to what the individual wants to do, before they've found out what exactly it is the individual wants to do. It was also playing for time. I hadn't been paying that much attention to the progress of the PDs. Obviously reading from notes, Haughey monotoned his way through a tour of the proud history and present-day vibrancy of the Fianna Fáil party. (Whenever Fianna Fáil talks about either vibrancy or vindication, it's a dead giveaway. They're goosed and they know it.)

'No,' I interrupted, suddenly certain. 'No, you won't say that.'

'I must send a strong message to the grassroots,' he responded.

'Frig the grassroots,' I said. 'The grassroots you always have with you. It's the waverers you have to reach today, and you're not going to reach them by making those kind of predictable threatened noises.'

With the infinite patience he could muster under pressure, he asked me what precisely I was recommending.

'No speech,' I said. 'No statement. You should arrive at the Burlo in high good humour. You shouldn't rush past them. Instead, you should get out of the car as if it was a surprise birthday party – pick off individual journalists you know in the crowd and tease them unmercifully, by name. Make the whole lot of them laugh and while they're laughing, wave and disappear into the hotel.'

'I would never do that.'

'Mr Haughey, you'll do whatever you decide. I'm just telling you what you *should* do.'

The conversation ended with a barely civil thank you from him and a banged-down phone. A few hours later, my assistant slid an evening paper in front of me. Big picture of the man, surrounded by microphone-holding journalists, with the caption 'An ebullient Charlie Haughey outside the Burlington Hotel today.'

'What's ebullient?' someone asked.

'Something good or Terry wouldn't be looking so relieved,' another staffer replied.

They were right. He had overcome his own preferences and gone for humour. The impact of Molloy's move could never be glossed over, but Haughey had at least stiffened his own party by appearing to be unbothered by this, the latest episode in a brilliantly planned wave. He never mentioned it to me afterwards and Tom never brought it up during any of their regular tea-fuelled meetings.

On one occasion, Tom was working with a group in the Mount Street headquarters of Fianna Fáil when Haughey arrived, courteously asking permission to interrupt the session. Tom stood back. Haughey told the group he had just made senators of two members of the party. The group applauded.

'That makes you the modern equivalent of Caligula,' Tom said, turning to resume the meeting.

'I'm not familiar with the classical reference, Tom.'

'Caligula made his horse a consul. Making those two boyos into senators is roughly the same thing.'

The group sat frozen. Haughey sat silent. Then he roared laughing. And then – only then – the group laughed, too. It was a chilling echo of the moment in the film *A Man for All Seasons* where Henry VIII, leaping from his boat, lands up to his knees in silt. The courtiers on the deck of the boat stand in terrified silence as he glares at them, daring them to disrespect him by as much as a snigger. Then the monarch himself decides to find the incident funny, throwing back his magnificent head in laughter. The courtiers all copy, not only his laughter, but his leap into the mud as well: they jump off the boat and splash about in the filth. That was the kind of effect Charles Haughey had, not by role but by force of personality.

Haughey was a medieval monarch out of time, defining the mood of his courtiers and, through them, the mood of the nation. Up to a point. The mood of the nation, during the Haughey years, was deeply split, with a sizable minority seeing him as a victim of everybody else, including perfidious Albion, with a majority regarding him as dislikeable, dangerous and probably corrupt.

6

Tips and Tricks

Outside politics, our market was expanding. Lawyers decided we had something to offer, following a pattern whereby we rarely spotted an opportunity until it found its own way to us, uninvited.

Solicitors and barristers came to us with all sorts of challenges. They had an upcoming trial which would require a doctor, architect or electrical engineer to provide their expertise to help the jury understand the alleged crime, but the doctor, architect or engineer they wanted to use needed to be upskilled and smartish, because otherwise they might be not a contribution to the case but a dire disadvantage. The lawyers knew what they wanted but could not train witnesses themselves. They could, however, tell us the rules they wanted followed, including how to sit, where to look and how to answer questions so as not to irritate the judge.

In order to get good at this, we had to learn the principles and practice of cross-examination, which added yet another strand to the corpus of knowledge represented by our growing library of communications books. Expert witness training became a regular part of our offering, with increasing numbers of medics, in particular, finding their way to us before they stepped into the witness box.

This kind of training was thrilling because of what we learned about what doctors and others are supposed to do, as compared with what a minority actually do. It also reinforced our understanding that communications is not a one-size-fits-all skill. Some expert witnesses were naturally terse. If they were asked a question, they answered yes or no. Some, on the other hand, were discursive, dying to be interesting. It took us a while to realise that the first kind tended to do better in court. Offering stuff you haven't been asked for, particularly if you're being cross-examined by the defence, is unwise. The rule of good radio and television – offer, offer, offer, offer – does not apply to court appearances.

Curiously, the other factor we noted, but rarely conveyed to trainees undergoing expert witness training, is that a big brain doesn't necessarily help. If, say, a woman was going to testify as to the misuse of a particular anaesthetic in an operating theatre, she might, as questioning progressed, identify where it was going and see dangers around the corner. If she was assertive as well as clever, she might seek to steer the interrogation in the right direction from her point of view, but this is not acceptable. Expert witness evidence-giving is not winning an argument, point by point, or making implications about the direction taken by the opposing counsel, so a witness who has only enough brain power to concentrate on their own data, which may be substantial, may actually be more effective than one with a wider brain power.

For the most part, the clients who used our services saw us as airline pilots see a flight simulator or aviation training device: a safe way to explore a stressful situation before it actually happens, and a method to develop skills in private. They wanted to know the rules governing everything from TV appearances to board meetings, from job interviews to chairing meetings, and how best to meet those rules.

A few, though, came to us with other agendas. Very soon, our trainers began to refer to one cluster as the Authentic Brigade. It was likely you'd get at least one on every group in an open course. Pleasant, clever, successful executives who had been sent by someone else, whether their boss, mentor or human resources manager, and who were not bought into the training in advance. On the contrary, as you'd find when you asked participants what they'd decided to achieve on the course. Well, this minority figure would say they had reservations. Oh yeah? About life, the universe and everything? Or something more specific? The thing is, they would tell us, they didn't want to be made inauthentic. Because they were authentic now. That was what they were.

We never said, 'You may be authentic, but your manners are lousy. By articulating your resentment at coming to an establishment you suspect, without evidence, is going to set out to confect you into something you're not, you have attributed spurious intent to us and insulted our professionalism. You've also not bothered your authentic arse to talk to anybody who has come through our process and we have severe doubts about whatever the hell you think constitutes this invaluable authenticity you claim.'

Instead, we asked more questions, and invariably the vague semi-accusation boiled down to a conviction on their part that preparing for any communication somehow falsified the person doing the communication. It was more authentic and you were a better person with more integrity if you went into the encounter as raw as a freshly snagged turnip.

In fairness, many current affairs broadcasters would buy into that belief. In an ideal world, they would love to see politicians arrive into their studios unprepared and untutored. They would claim that this makes the politicians more authentic, although it is difficult to imagine another profession where coming unprepared to a crucial encounter can be construed as positive.

A lovely example of preparedness in play and journalistic resentfulness of same happened in 2018, when *Sunday Times* columnist David Quinn tweeted this:

The built world around you; men did that. Your house, car, street, plumbing, electric wiring, etc. Men. Let's say something nice about men today.

On Virgin's *Tonight Show*, Anton Savage reacted negatively to this, offering Mr Quinn, a fellow panellist, another scenario.

If you were to take a plane – 25 per cent built by women – to fly to Manhattan, for instance, and stride out into Times Square and say 'Isn't this amazing? Skyscrapers, subways, Central Park, Park Avenue, all built by white people. Aren't white people marvellous?' people would say 'Hang on a minute. That is deliberately exclusionary, reactionary and ignores the fact that you disenfranchised all other races for a millennium. The same is true in Ireland. You picked the only industry that women no longer have any role in and used that as your selection to praise men. Why didn't you use medicine? Why didn't you use pharmaceuticals? Why didn't you use veterinary science? Why didn't you use any of those where there is a representation of women? And not only that, you had to curate's-egg it –

At this point, Quinn interrupted.
'You've obviously rehearsed this,' he retorted.
'Well, I gave it some thought – something you didn't do,' was the response.
The encounter was palpably won because one of the panellists had – irritatingly to the other – carefully prepared. Nobody, however, could suggest that the preparation made him inauthentic. And that's the reality of preparing and rehearsing key communications. It is an opportunity to be more, rather than less, authentic. It is a chance to reach into your own experience, your own background, your own reference points in order to illustrate the point you want to leave in the memory of your audience.

The problem, even in the 1980s, was that people without an understanding of media training were setting up to do it. Inevitably, because many of them had been journalists or broadcasters or both, they knew what they would want to hear from a politician in response to the obvious questions, and so they would tell the politician what he or she should say. They would – and still do – put words into the politician's mouth. It never struck them that this was to falsify the politician and to reinforce their belief that media preparation would set out to make them less authentic.

In addition to the participants who perceived training to be a threat to their unalloyed genuineness, and probably outnumbering them, were those who had damn all interest in the truthfulness of their presentation and who wanted tips and tricks. They did not care about getting ideas from their heads into the heads of voters or constituents, possibly in some cases because ideas would not have been that numerous in their heads. What they wanted was insider trading: the secrets that would make them seem better than they were, more powerful, more lucid and more charming. They had heard that certain gestures were used by winners, and they wanted to be taught those gestures. They had read that certain words made you sound more energetic or driven, and they wanted the list to learn off. They had been told that smiling when you spoke made you more relatable – they just wanted to know the best conversational place in which to insert a grin.

Some of the tips they wanted were a logical extension of anxiety. Some people, for example, who use reading glasses and might need them in order to quote from a document, would ask for advice: should they put them on and take them off or leave them on all the time, even if they blurred the presenter's face? That's legitimate. The approach tried out by a medical consultant with me one day is not.

He had flown in – from Canada, I think – to give himself a couple of days to get over jet lag while preparing for his interview for a post as consultant in his speciality in one of the acute hospitals. As requested, he emailed his CV before the day of the first preparatory interview, and when I printed it out, I figured that unless he had major one-to-one communications problems, the consultancy was in his back pocket. He was that impressive.

The morning I interviewed him was something of a disappointment. He was fidgety and imprecise, taking longer to get to the point in response to questions than he should have. It was about a 70 per cent performance. When we moved to playback and assessment, he became even more fidgety, to such an extent that I thought he might have a neurological problem. Taking a risk, I stopped the recording.

'What the hell are you doing?' I asked him.

Unexpectedly, he glowed and smiled.

'I'm mirroring,' he told me.

'You're what?'

'Mirroring. Neuro-linguistic programming. When one person mirrors the way another person moves, it creates a bond between them.'

Now I got it. During the interview and as we began the playback, he was seeking to sit in the same position as me, put his hands where I put mine, tilt his head whichever way I tilted mine. Because I had to cope with recording, checking sound, skipping back and forth through his CV, drinking water and jotting notes, he had a great deal of action to follow. Consequentially his fidgeting and distraction from what he needed to communicate. He had also, I suspected, confused cause and effect. When people bond, when couples fall in love, they tend to sit in a way that favours the other and probably – without realising what they're at – mimic the other person's movements. But it's a result of the bonding, of the mutual affection, rather than a cause of it. In addition, trying to make someone like you more by mimicking them is a tad manipulative. Because he was so clever, he copped on quickly that he was doing himself no favours and we were able to concentrate on data, thus freeing himself to be his authentic best self and get the job.

The market for tricks never diminishes. Something about a secret cunning method intrigues even folk who are normally straightforward and honourable. Once they believe they're rare, if not unique, in knowing about the secret, they swallow it, hook, line and sinker.

Take the lying thing. HR people, other job interviewers and broadcasters are often convinced that they can spot when the person they're interrogating is lying. Why? One of the reasons is that they run an index finger around their collar. Or they get sweaty. Or they put a hand over their mouth while talking: that's a dead giveaway.

An American named Stan B. Walters encountered the same conviction among police officers when he did some research into how good they were at spotting liars in action. He found that police officers – and, later, FBI agents – were convinced that they were particularly good at spotting the physical 'tells' revealing that someone was telling porkies. Not so, he discovered. Neither professional group was more than marginally better at spotting untruths than were members of the general public. Walters then took the individuals' 'tells' and worked out that although they frequently appeared during interrogations, they were often caused by the anxiety of the innocent finding themselves in a terrifying situation, rather than by guilt. The more practised a criminal, the less likely they were to use these supposedly 'giveaway' gestures. (In the same way, it's been found that when held for questioning, the innocent are the ones who pace their cell and wring their hands, whereas the guilty go to sleep.)

All of which is not to deny that media training is available that actively seeks to confect the subject into someone more relatable, more quotable, more knowledgeable than they are, and sets out to do it through tricks. My company never offers tricks. The only time I can remember when we used something that could be described as a trick was during a European Parliament election, when some of my staff came to me with a problem. The candidate could acquit himself creditably enough when it came to standing up and emitting words. That wasn't the problem. The problem was that many of the public meetings he was required to attend took the form of the candidates seated in a row facing the audience, whether in the local basketball court or school hall. Because a fair number of candidates were involved, this entailed sitting still for some time while each was called to the podium or, later, asked a question. Our man was falling asleep.

Which, given that he was facing the audience, was not helpful. Could I think of anything that might prevent somnolence?

Actually, I could. Because my wonderful husband could go to sleep at any moment without provocation, his son had likened him to the dormouse in *Alice's Adventures in Wonderland*. Throughout our lives together, I lived in terror that when he drove to Louth to see family members, he would fall asleep at the wheel. Then I found a gadget in America that looked like a big old-fashioned hearing aid and had been invented for long-distance truckers. If you wore it while driving and started to drop off, your head would naturally tip forward, the gadget would sense the movement and would scream in your ear, waking you up. My husband, when presented with this useful purchase, told me where to stick it, and it sat in a junk drawer for several years before the sleepy candidate appeared. I handed it over, he wore it and – although it was somewhat outside my job description as a political communications trainer – the problem was solved.

7

POLITICAL COMMUNICATIONS MOVE CENTRE STAGE

One of the key talents a politician can possess is shutting up. Politicians love to share and have other people share, and it's not always useful to their career. Witness President Jimmy Carter and the rabbit. Carter was out fishing when he encountered a swamp rabbit which didn't think much of him and swam pretty aggressively towards his boat. A photograph was taken at the time.

Carter wasn't in any way damaged by the rabbit and it wasn't that exciting an encounter, but he told some of his staff in the White House and when they weren't impressed, because, honestly, the breast-stroking animal in the photograph wasn't exactly the King Kong of the rabbit kingdom, Carter got shirty and ordered the picture to be blown up, so they could see it in all its threatening glory. Inevitably, with a few scoops in them, his press people then passed on the details of the rabbit saga to their press colleagues, and in no time the president being attacked by a rampant rabbit was all over the media. Had he been popular at the time, this might have deepened his popularity, but he wasn't, and that swamp rabbit dogged him (pardon the expression) for the remainder of his period in office.

'Loose lips sink ships,' was the British slogan carried on posters in buses and trains during the Second World War in an effort to get the owners of those loose lips to get a grip of their potentially damaging blather. It's a useful piece of advice in political terms, too. Fewer journalists are permanent and pensionable these days; many of them are supplying multiple platforms. This means that the competition between them, the competition to survive, is more pressing than at any time in the past. That is complicated by the fact that politicians, like the rest of us, suffer from acute fear of missing out, or FOMO, which makes them answer almost any phone call, even from unidentified numbers. It is further complicated by ministers and ministers of state having media advisers, who necessarily engage in transactionism with hacks of all kinds: you give me a steer on this one and I'll be less than vicious about your woman when she next cocks up.

In the pre-TV/radio past, secrets could be kept for ever. The secrecy time span shortened with electronic media, and has been cut to nothing in the last ten years, with more leaks than a colander and with politicians talking when they should shut up. My company has frequently advised politicians of different parties not to go on radio or TV when they clearly haven't mastered their subject matter, knowing that they will do no service to the public if they do. I can remember literally no case where this advice was taken. Either the politician was convinced that everybody would find them guilty of something if they didn't broadcast, or the word came down from the party leader to get themselves into a studio chair that day, never mind the consequences.

The standards and imperatives of print media have changed utterly, too. Although US papers did once run a picture of Lyndon B. Johnson lifting up one of his dogs by the ears, they mostly kept quiet about his crudity about other people, particularly women. This was a man who would conduct meetings with subordinates while seated on the toilet doing what 'seated on the toilet' implies. But just as they had kept to themselves what they knew about JFK's philandering, they continued to kid themselves that self-censorship about Johnson was in the interest of respect for the role. It was the culture of the time.

Then came Watergate, which changed how journalists saw themselves. Ben Bradley, editor of the *Washington Post*, became a global household name standing for press freedom and efficacy. Never mind that he had a questionable past with the Kennedys, who used him as a sounding board for nascent policies, knowing that he'd be flattered by being called to the White House late in the evening for face-to-face encounters with the president, and also glad of advance notice on emerging directions. That was forgotten because of Watergate, which turned Bradley into a secular saint and a generation of students into aspirant Woodwards and Bernsteins.

All this upped the importance of media skills for politicians in the US and Europe. And that was before the election of 'the Great Communicator', Ronald Reagan, now remembered as the warm, accessible, kindly figure he most certainly was not, as evidenced by his response to a famous ransom case of the time.

American heiress Patty Hearst had a bad day in February 1974 when a small leftist group calling themselves the Symbionese Liberation Army grabbed the 19-year-old college student and held her hostage, demanding that her family give food to the poor. The Hearsts distributed $2m worth of food. The then governor of California's reaction? 'It's just too bad we can't have an epidemic of botulism.'

In other words, the then future US president was so bothered by the very idea of the poor getting free food, he would have been happy to have them coincidentally poisoned. The temptation is to see that statement as an aberration, the untypical outburst of a man under pressure – not like the constant awful emissions of the present president. Not so. In fact, Reagan's statements parallel those of Trump to an eerie extent.

Let's start, in this instance, by looking at Trump. Take the performance on 16 March 2024 in Dayton, Ohio, where Trump made a speech described by journalist Michael Wolff in *All or Nothing*, his book on how Trump recaptured America, as replete with 'particularly concentrated hortatory language from Trump of the most malevolent kind'.

'Now, if I don't get elected, it's gonna be a bloodbath. That's going to be the least of it. It's going to be bloodbath for the country.' That is what he said.

He predicted, rather than actually called for, a bloodbath. That is the difference between Trump and Reagan. As governor of California, the latter actively wished death on college campus demonstrators: 'If it's to be a bloodbath, let it be now.'

But the likeness goes further. Trump's random connection to facts and truth was probably exceeded by Reagan's. Robert Scheer, clinical professor of communications at the University of Southern California, has noted that

> [Reagan] would continue to use erroneous information with crowds, even after he had been told it was wrong. For example, his claim that a government study showed that Alaska had greater oil potential than the known reserves of Saudi Arabia. Those of us travelling with him soon discovered that he had got the report wrong, and press aide Jim Lake conceded it. But Reagan had grown too fond of the line to drop it and claimed to his aides that it was based on a newspaper clipping that he had picked up somewhere but could no longer find.

So what is the qualitative difference, then, between presidents Trump and Reagan?

The late Norman Corwin, in his seminal 1983 examination of – as its title explained – *Trivializing America*, wrote of Reagan:

> If ever there was a pygmy in giant shoes, it is this man, who has no apparent grace or talent beyond being able to read a script with the competence of a professional actor, the glibness of a preposterous businessman discussing politics at a dinner party, an all-purpose utilitarian smile, a nicely groomed smartness at saluting military persons, and an air of confidence that he cuts an admirable figure in his entrances and exits. He is endowed

with neither a keen wit nor a gift of language, and he has only the vaguest sense of history. He is unlettered in art and science and waddles like a stegosaur in economics, but worst of all, he is a man without the slightest humility or compassion.

What protected Reagan was his innate likeability. Voters and the media liked him. TV current affairs producers found that, even when they were running stories about bad housing start-ups. Footage of the president on a building site, wearing a hard hat and joshing with construction workers, served to mock the negative story the reporter was articulating at the time. Plus, nothing was ever his fault. *Playboy* magazine noted his phenomenal capacity to blame others. Donald Trump is his good student when it comes to blame distribution.

Yet the memory of Reagan, even in Ireland, is infused with the belief that he was a great communicator and basically a good guy. He was neither. The communications myth developed because he was a professional actor who knew how to deliver a good line, like the one he came out with when he was asked if he was too old for the White House: 'I am not going to exploit for political purposes my opponent's youth and inexperience.' Great line, prepared by some copy-writer and superbly delivered. Anyone tempted to do the same with an Irish politician should remember that not one of them, presently, is a trained actor. Reagan didn't just deliver individual lines crafted by others. He knew how to deliver a great script, and he got one of them after another from his wonderful speechwriter Peggy Noonan.

He also had, we must admit, a trait every politician needs: knowing when not to take ostensibly good advice from experts. Ed Rollins, a man who advised more than one Republican US president, noted, with curled lip, that his handlers wasted much time 'trying to explain television to a guy who didn't need any tips'.

In a mock session … the president insisted on looking at his interlocutors when he answered a question. Roger Ailes, one of the best in the business, insisted that he should be looking directly into the television camera.

'Don't you think,' the president asked in exasperation, 'that people will think I'm a phony if I don't look at the people who are talking to me?'

Ailes insisted. For the rest of the rehearsal, the president looked squarely at the camera.

During the actual debate, on the other hand, he went with his instincts and ignored the high-priced advice. He looked reporters square in the eye as he answered their questions. 'He always knew an audience better than any of us.'

Another adviser who went on to become a TV presenter and commentator, George Stephanopoulos, later wrote about the 'perverse pleasure' of recorded rehearsals in advance of big outings.

> You got to put your boss on the spot while telling yourself it was for his own good: 'Governor [Bill] Clinton, electing a president is ultimately a matter of trust, and polls show that the American people just don't trust you. What's your response?' Silence. His eyes would become slits, and his lips would disappear. 'So what do you want me to say,' he would finally reply in a voice muted by contempt. You could almost hear the next word: 'Smartass.'

Media training isn't fun, nor should it be. In consequence, many people – including journalists – who undergo basic training never return. They may improve, but it wasn't fun and afterwards they think they are done and dusted, which is a big mistake, because media changes all the time and a dated method is a turn-off. One example is the presenter who is so impressed by the research handed to them that they feel the need to incorporate thick slices of it in every question. It's easy to spot this happening because the interviewee's answer is 'Absolutely.' They have, in other words, been handed a thesis dressed up as a question and can think of no better response than confirmation.

I have worked, particularly in advance of Big Debates, with perhaps ten political leaders. None of them bounced in, gleeful at the prospect of doing a simulated version of what they would later have to do for real. One of the most studious of them, the Fianna Fáil leader and current Taoiseach, Micheál Martin, would start ratty and get rattier as the process continued. I don't mean he was ratty at me or anybody else in studio. Nor was he ratty at his own staff or even at himself. Micheál Martin does an impressive undirected ratty when rehearsing, like a good actor working on a show that hasn't hit the stage yet.

Watching him during one Big Debate prep taught me its purpose. When you're the consultant in this situation, you're not there to catch them doing something wrong and tell them off for it. You *are* there, as Tom Savage always dictated, to catch them doing something right and help them incorporate that into their essentials for the evening. But most of all, you're a catalyst rather than a participant, and this requires the subordination of your ego – we'll come back to that. You're a catalyst creating a situation during which the leader hears themselves saying stuff. It may be the first time they've heard themselves articulate a particular point, and if they're Micheál Martin, they see it on playback and don't need you to stop it because they're already reacting to it. The shaken head, the wincing facial expression. The silent mouthing of the words they said on screen but now know are not quite right. It's the old 'How do I know what I think until I hear what I say?' rule playing out in front of you, and it is marvellous to watch. Marvellous and properly humbling, because what you are watching is all about them and precious little about you. You're seeing them examining the unexamined, refreshing their personal clichés, groping for the illustration that will make a particular point 'sticky'.

Initially, in Big Debate preparation, you are a catalyst, but as the session progresses, when you're working with a brilliant, experienced politician, your role is reduced to that of a witness, as you observe the man or woman doing their own work, making their own decisions. Some politicians will flag you to stop the playback, think for a while, then ask you what you think of an alternative statement. You listen and may comment, but you know, as they finish saying it, that they have made up their own mind.

You may have a small function in helping a leader to avoid personal habits like the over-use of conceptual language, for example, but mainly, the function of Big Debate rehearsal is to help them clear their mind, prioritise what they need to present to the viewer/listener, choose their own evidence and get over the inevitably negative questions from the chair.

Questions a broadcaster asks a politician are always negative, because the broadcaster doesn't want to sound like they're part of the politician's PR team. In a properly managed Big Debate, the broadcaster is scrupulously obeying rules set down by their employer and by Comisiún na Meán, ensuring that each participant gets roughly the same amount of time and is asked to cover more or less the same territory. More political parties in the Houses of the Oireachtas means more claims to participate and less of the drama of the direct head-to-heads we saw in the past with Garret and Charlie. Indeed, for some stations, the commentary afterwards about how each leader performed may be more interesting than the Big Debate itself.

8

Lochinvar

We had first encountered Pádraig Flynn at the media skills course where Tom had enjoined him to silence except when recording an exercise. Thereafter, in the year when I was in the post-crash wheelchair, Flynn would drop into the Old Railway Station, uninvited, so you'd find him making tea in the kitchen; or he would ask me to come to meetings in Leinster House, where he would have arranged a ground-floor meeting room and would be on the watch for my white Civic with the long doors, all the better to get a wheelchair in and out from behind the driver's seat. Flynn would take out the wheelchair, get it ready, hold it still while I got into it, take my keys, lock the car and push the wheelchair like a professional carer.

Other than appreciating his wheelchair skills, I didn't know what to make of him. In background and geography, we had nothing in common, as he constantly reminded me, telling me my views were 'Dublin 4', even though I was from Dublin 3. I was married to an ex-priest and was socially liberal. He was extremely committed to his Catholic faith and widely regarded as in the front line of social conservatism. Many of the political correspondents ignored or shrugged him off as a throwback who was going nowhere, greatly helped in this by a behaviour pattern of his: when engaging with an individual or group who didn't know him, he would approach, chest advanced, proper physical distancing unobserved, putting on an accent stronger than his normal west of Ireland accent and challenging them on something irrelevant. It took a while for me to realise that what he was at was intelligence-testing on the hoof. If a newcomer, faced with the yokel performance, decided this minister was a gobshite, then the minister had the measure of the newcomer. The newcomer, on the other hand, didn't have the measure of the minister. Only a few – notably journalistic colleagues Gerald Barry and Vincent Browne – found this introductory performance amusing and had an appreciation that behind it was a big brain and interesting complexities.

At a time when Fianna Fáil tacitly approved of CJ's marital infidelity, Flynn was convinced – and tried to convince me – that it could not be true. When he eventually realised it *was* true, he was saddened. He was absolute in his fealty to his own wife, Dorothy, a Dublin doctor's daughter, having distinguished himself in the worst way to her family by falling into their Christmas tree early on. He always protected women who worked for him from any possibility of personal invasion – the too-close squaring-up thing he did was inflicted only on men. If you were a woman working for Pádraig Flynn, he would not touch you or inflict random hugs on you or make comments about what you were wearing. This despite his capacity to accurately state any woman's bra size, which emerged by accident one day. Those of us present were particularly intrigued by this, partly because of his consistent respectful distancing from women, partly because it surfaced almost like a claim to a professional skill. When someone made that point to him, he got quite offended and said it *was* a professional skill; that his family had generations in the drapery business and he could tell you anybody's measurements on sight to within an inch or so. He could also identify the constitution of any fabric, stating that pure new wool should always have a small percentage of an artificial fabric in it in order to help the garment hold its shape. He loved Travellers and was hugely proud of having set up the first school for Traveller children.

He painted with considerable skill. He was a bravura singer of 'The West's Awake'.

When Charlie Haughey formed his new cabinet in March 1987, I was done with the wheelchair and my memory had improved enough for me to go back to training. On this day I was finishing a training programme in Boston, when, in the middle of playback, Bill Fitzgerald, the big man running the course, came into the room and told me 'The Irish Minister for the Environment is on the phone for you.' Since it was coming up to coffee break anyway, I followed Bill, asking him if the caller had by any chance given his name. Bill shrugged, looking mildly surprised that I didn't already know it. I lifted the phone and gave a cautious, generic greeting.

'Come home,' said Flynn's voice.

I congratulated him on achieving a senior ministry in a big-spending department.

'Never mind that. Come home. You will be my adviser. I'm in trouble. I've closed down several state bodies, including An Foras Forbartha, and I have to go on *Morning Ireland* and defend the decision.'

Talking quickly because I didn't want to keep my course participants waiting, I told him that first of all, he should not go on the programme with the intention of doing PR for any action he was taking. If he believed he had done the right thing and had cabinet support for it, he should begin by giving the data, then explain the data and answer every question truthfully, rather than trying to minimise the pain he was causing. He was not to spin. I told him I would be in the Custom House before lunchtime the following day – I was due to fly out that night anyway. Good, he said, he would show me my new office. Then he put down the phone. I stood in a borrowed Boston office, wanting to tell my mother, who had once worked in the Custom House, what he had just told me. Imagine: I was going to have my own office there. I got a grip on my notions and hurried back to the course.

At home the next morning, having showered and diluted my jet lag with strong coffee, I listened as Tom played the recorded *Morning Ireland*. On the programme, the presenter started at high doh with a first question that went something like 'Minister, the first thing you did was to close down An Foras Forbartha, and you gave them twenty-four hours' notice!'

'No', came the truthful reply, 'I gave them twelve hours' notice.'

Later that day, I went into the Custom House, vaguely remembering seeing as a child, from the top deck of a bus, children from the inner city swimming in the angular pool dominated by a statue in the grounds of what I believe to be the most beautiful building in Dublin. Inside, it was brown-linoed and old-fashioned, including the small office, three doors down from the minister's, where I would be based. He introduced me to his private secretary, Gerry Rice, yelling at him to put on a jacket, which Gerry did, winking at me while he did it and telling me his last job as an air traffic controller in Dublin airport hadn't been anything like as stressful as this one was shaping up to be. Paradoxically, Gerry seemed quite happy at the prospect. It was obvious that within hours of Flynn's appointment the two of them already had an amused and amusing partnership going. It was always the same with Pádraig Flynn. His staff adored him. They adored him because he was clever and hardworking, for starters. But also because when something went wrong, he never spread the blame. He was the minister, he was responsible and he was the one to blame, no matter how bad the error. His staff adored him, too, because of his steady mood. He was always in good humour. Even if he was having a pitched battle with you, he was good-humoured about it. He had that rare ability to be able to break away from whatever serious task he was at to have a few minutes of banter and a bit of skit and then switch right back to the serious stuff. Because Flynn liked the job and liked the people working for him, the people working for him became a team of friends and those friendships continued long after we were spun loose from the central connection.

We were new to him and he was new to being a minister. But that didn't intimidate him. When directing the first official photo shoot, I ticked off the shots we were required to have, and then said to him that after the more formal ones, it would be good to have a few of him in shirtsleeves. If I had suggested he dance naked for the camera, it couldn't have been less welcome. 'Nobody but Dorothy has ever seen me in my shirtsleeves,' he told me. 'And nobody ever will.' He believed that dressing impeccably was a duty for a public figure, and he was contemptuous of politicians or public servants who, in wardrobe or grooming terms, were slobs.

Pádraig Flynn was one of the few politicians with whom I have worked who didn't do 'over-the-wall' communication. 'Over-the-wall' communication started in the Ford Motor Company when the Edsel was being created. This car, designed to be a homage to Edsel, the dead son of founder Henry Ford, was sketched out by a designer who effectively threw the drawings over the wall to the engineers, who worked out where the piping had to go, then they threw it over the wall to the next team and finally the thing was thrown over another wall to the marketing and communications people with the instruction to make the American people like this car. This was an impossible ask, because the car was a dog in every respect. However, the need for communications people to be in at the ground level of any big decisions has still not got through to many big public bodies and private industries, who see their PR and communications people as soft and fuzzy rather than functional, and who, when the shit hits the fan, decide, like the chief executive of Enron, that it's a communications issue, which it isn't, and call in the PR people.

Flynn irritated his senior civil servants by involving me at the point where policy was being envisioned. I remember a discussion about the possibility of DuPont, the American chemical giant, building an incinerator on the border to service the North and the Republic. A provably good idea, given both the willingness of DuPont to put its money where its mouth was and the possibility of cross-border functioning. Each of the four men around the table presented their thinking to the minister, who then asked me, formally, for my input. (He always addressed me, in a group, as 'Miss Prone' and referred to me in my absence as 'The Lady'. It underlined an aspect of the job I am ashamed to admit gave me enormous pleasure. Being the only woman in the room did that. It rarely, if ever, happens the younger generations of women.)

I referred to all the points made earlier in the meeting, and then said that, given the negative public perception of incineration at the time (the early eighties) there wasn't a snowball's chance in hell that the incinerator would become a reality. The civil servants were shocked and furious. I suggested that some objective research be done into public opinion. That didn't happen, because the project had taken on the cast of the fatally walking wounded and quickly died. Even civil servants who liked me believed I should have been brought in months or years later, to produce beautiful videos and craft ministerial speeches to persuade the people of Ireland that this was a good thing.

It wasn't the only time we diverged in our valorising of communications versus other forms of action. Another occasion was when I was invited to be present during presentation pitches by three advertising agencies tendering for the job of persuading Irish people to opt for unleaded petrol. Countless studies had proved that lead in petrol got into the atmosphere and did grievous damage to the growing brains of children, particularly children in cities. It was imperative, then, to move petrol consumption away from leaded (lead prevented engines developing a 'knock'), but Ireland was lagging behind other European Community countries and was likely to be fined if we didn't get our act together. So a few senators, civil servants and I got to watch the rough drafts of different imaginative approaches to effecting that change, and then joined the minister in his office. This time, he came to me first.

'All three were excellent. Creative, well-researched, beautifully executed,' I said.

'And?'

'And I wouldn't use any of them. You have a budget coming up in six weeks' time. If, in that budget, you drop the price of unleaded petrol noticeably below the price of leaded petrol, that'll do the trick.'

Flynn did an open-handed gesture at the others and met with a flustered silence. Each had made careful objective notes of the merits of the presentations and none was expecting the issue to be upended. One of them humorously said something to the effect that he disapproved of communications people contributing to policy-making because it was neither their job nor their competence, but in this instance ... Six weeks later, that's what happened. A major switchover in fuel use promptly happened and Ireland was back in good nick with the European Community.

When it came to speeches, Flynn was a mixed joy to write for. He was a joy because he didn't want regulation ministerial speeches. They're the ones that start with a couple of sentences in Irish and end with a couple more sentences in Irish. Flynn's Irish was fluent and beautiful to listen to, like Geoghegan-Quinn's, but he knew – as did she – that ritual early and late token use of Irish was a dud, dated formula.

The other characteristic of a standard ministerial speech, then and now, is that it carries no trace of the speaker. It is, as my Tom used to say, 'moving bones from one graveyard to another', the bones being facts and expenditure. Ministers love to tell the public how much money the government is spending on them. Never mind that it's the public's money in the first place. The difference between features and benefits, between the bald facts of expenditure and the human difference that expenditure will make, isn't understood by many politicians, but Flynn got it early. He was always willing to sit down, about a week before a speech was to be delivered, to lay out his thinking on an issue, or where he had encountered the problem or challenge before. He would frequently quote poetry in Irish, using the language in a natural way in the course of an oration. His fellow Mayo man, Enda Kenny, had the same facility, and not just with poetry. When Enda hit a point in a speech or a piece to camera in which he was particularly invested, he was likely to break into Irish, which was grand, except for Diarmuid O'Grady, the wonderful SpeechCue operator who would be feeding the words of the agreed speech through to the two screens seen by Enda. Diarmuid is not a fluent Irish speaker, and so broke out in a cold sweat whenever Enda segued into Irish, because Diarmuid had no idea where or if Enda would go back to the original speech in English.

Once I had done the research and knew how Flynn felt about an issue, I would go away and craft a speech. In the beginning, he would read through it aloud to catch any usage or phraseology that wasn't natural to him. As time went on, however, and trust built up between us, he decided he didn't need to go through the caper of reading it out loud before setting off. Sure, it would be fine. He'd get plenty of time to read it in the ministerial Merc on the way to the venue. Of course he would. Except of course he never did, because of phone calls involving one or other of his two mobile phones. And so Minister Flynn would arrive at an international housing conference or seminar about pollution, script in hand, having not given it a glance throughout the journey. He would then stand up, slide the paper clip off the pages, and sight-read the thing flawlessly. It was always a tour de force and audiences loved it, looking for copies of the oration afterwards, but it filled me with terror that I would accidentally include an error that he would put on the national record. In fact, I once did that. He and his minister of state, Mary Harney, were at daggers drawn over legislation to curb the appalling smog in our cities. Even though it was Harney's initiative and legislation, Flynn, as the cabinet minister, was the one to introduce it in the Dáil, so I wrote the minister's speech, handed it over and moved on to something else. I was fortunate that copies of ministerial speeches are distributed in Leinster House minutes before the minister involved stands up to deliver them. One of the porters, clutching a spare copy, accosted Flynn at the last minute before he went to his front-bench seat. 'Minister, are you sure you want to say this?' the porter asked. Flynn demanded to know what he was talking about and the porter stood beside him, pointing his ballpoint pen at the offending line: 'As of today, it will be illegal to sell or use smokeless fuel in Dublin.' Flynn was never going to ask the porter what was wrong with that, but after a couple of concentrated, eyes-narrowed seconds, he got it. It should have referred to 'smoky' fuel. Flynn asked the porter to bring it to the attention of his private secretary, who would correct copies for release to the media and others, and then marched into the chamber to disappoint members of the Opposition, and some of his own party, too, who had spotted the error and were just aching to have him say it on the floor of the house.

Having done it once, I constantly feared I might do it again and, anyway, it wasn't good enough, I decided, for the minister to endanger himself in this way, so I would have to teach him a lesson and get him to mend his ways. I crafted a speech for him, and around page three, found a logical way to insert this halfway down the page:

Question: How do hedgehogs make love?
Answer: Very carefully.

Flynn's driver later confirmed to me that the minister had not read his script before arriving at the venue. Instead, he did his usual thing of setting it up on the podium and launching into it. Turning from page two to page three, he somehow managed to spot the hedgehogs screwing away in the middle of the page and, even more impressively, managed to leap over them without losing the sense of the speech.

Only once did he get fidgety about a speech. The third time he checked a detail about that speech with me, I suggested he was worried and wondered why. The answer was a confirmation. Yes, he was seriously worried about it for the good reason that it was about depression and he had no experience of depression. No matter what happened him or what mistakes he made, then or later, he might experience regret or remorse, but never depression, and he was expending unusual concentration on making sure he knew what he was saying and knew that it would not offend someone who might have suffered from depression.

The only time I was in the Flynn home in Castlebar, it was like stepping into a different world, coming, as I did, from a non-political family. On the way there from Knock airport, I pointed to a boutique in the main street, saying that it looked very elegant. 'I wouldn't ever have been in that one,' Dorothy said. I was surprised. Flynn checked which shop was being talked about. 'That's a Blueshirt boutique,' he announced. I laughed and then realised he was serious. He named off all the political affiliations of the shops and coffee shops as we passed them. I was gobsmacked. As we turned on to the road to his home, he added that Castlebar had a Fine Gael undertaker *and* a Fianna Fáil undertaker.

The Flynn house is an elegant mansion and the lunch was superb, Dorothy being an excellent cook. In the middle of that Sunday lunch, however, people came up the path and knocked at the window and each time Flynn excused himself and went to deal with whatever it was they wanted. That was how local politics was done in Mayo and that's the way he did it.

When he became European Commissioner, he did the same thing at pan-European level, teasing and bellowing and doing deals. He also, as time went on, developed a more nuanced set of attitudes. In the early days as Commissioner, he would have been negative about homosexuality. By the time AIDS was laying waste to a generation of young men, he had changed so radically that in his first year as Commissioner, he sent out Valentine's Day cards with condoms attached, to hammer home the importance of safe sex. None of which made any difference to the way influential journalists back in Ireland regarded him. Once a stereotype, always a stereotype.

I remember ringing him before he came home from Brussels for some event to warn him that some of the hacks were working up to asking him questions about the improbable colour of his hair. What would he say, I asked, if that happened? 'I'll say isn't it wonderful that we all live in an era of choice,' he responded without hesitation. (In the event, nobody asked him, which was a disappointment.) Not long after that, a woman working in his Brussels office had a significant home hair dye disaster, the morning after which she sat at her desk, in the Commissioner's arrival path, wondering if he would comment. Of course he would. He marched past her, greeting her. Stopped. Reversed. Said 'Touché!' and walked on.

One-to-one, Pádraig Flynn is a different man from the public-arena Flynn. He is thoughtful, intellectually speculative, observant, and the best analyst of political processes you could ever find.

This is the point where a reader who knows the Flynn story will expect his disasters to be addressed. They are in the public domain and every negative comment possible has been made down through the years. I write about the man I worked for. Who – as others who worked for him would confirm – was a cavalcade of humour, outrageousness, insight and ideas.

9

The Drift

Within the inner circle of Fianna Fáil, it took a long time for Haughey's most faithful faithful, including Pádraig Flynn, to break ranks. Charlie McCreevy did it early and often, but what became pejoratively known as the 'Country & Western Alliance' – Máire Geoghegan-Quinn, Albert Reynolds and Pádraig Flynn – stayed on his front bench and remained ostensibly loyal for some years, although they became less happy towards the end of his period in power.

In common with many other politicians in Fine Gael, Fianna Fáil and Labour, Geoghegan-Quinn entered politics on the death of her father, Johnny Geoghegan. He had been a TD for Galway West for 21 years. Máire had trained as a primary school teacher, but, at twenty-four, she contested the by-election, took his seat and entered the Dáil in 1975. She served as parliamentary secretary to Des O'Malley, who ensured that when she returned to the House after the birth of her first son she was given a room where she could breastfeed her baby – something of a benign anomaly in the seventies. She was not an early Haughey supporter, voting for George Colley in 1979 after discussing the leadership with Des O'Malley. Despite that, Haughey appointed her to his cabinet, making her the first female minister since Constance Markievicz.

Tom Savage interviewing Bunny and Joan Carr for his TV series *For Better or Worse*

Terry – appointed to the Independent Radio and Television Commission by Ray Burke, who was later to personify a Tom Savage red line with Albert Reynolds

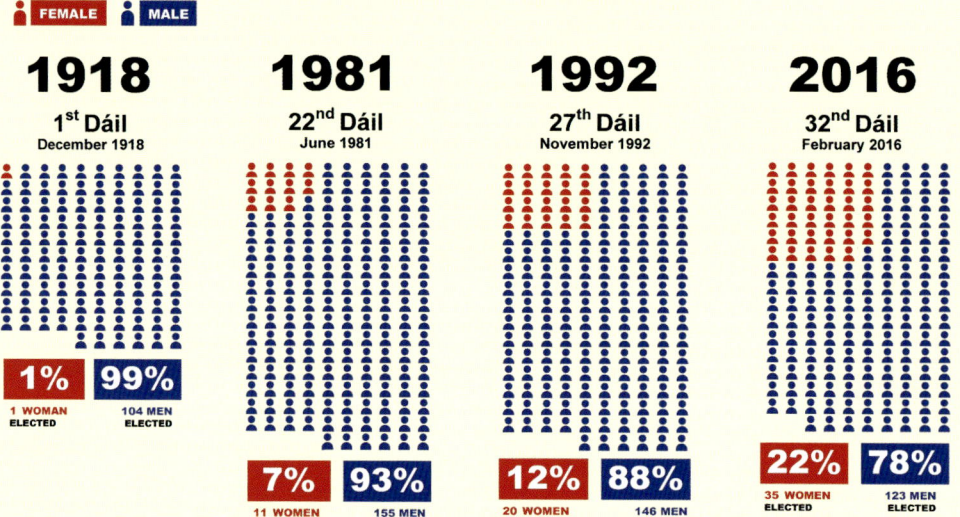

Women in Parliament – percentage of women and men elected to Dáil Éireann 1918–2018, © Houses of the Oireachtas 2017, Designed by: Oireachtas Library & Research Service

Terry training Eastern European women politicians in media skills in a course organised by Gemma Hussey

'Wearing a forced smile of abject gratitude.' Tony Gregory posing with Charles Haughey to mark the 'Gregory Deal'. © The *Irish Times*/Peter Thursfield, used with permission.

Close friends and colleagues – Máire Geoghegan-Quinn and the late Noel Treacy
© Getty Images, used with permission

Gerry Barry – the only journalist to spot the significance of Máire Geoghegan-Quinn's ard fheis tribute to CJ – with Tom Savage in the RTE newsroom

Seán Doherty with Charley Haughey, © Derek Speirs, reproduced with permission

'Fianna Fail must have contemporary objectives and be able to paint, for the public, a picture of the Ireland we should have in the year 2025' — Padraig Flynn

The future of Fianna Fail

By Padraig Flynn TD

IT'S AS simple as this:

If something is not done — and done quickly — then the most influential and representative political party in the history of the state will be critically weakened.

If something is not done — and done comprehensively — then Fianna Fail is heading for a century in which the Party will get steadily smaller and poorer.

If something is not done — and done collectively — then young Fianna Fail members will face years of opposition of coalition.

At this point the debilitation has gone so far and morale is so low, that immediate action is needed.

In the last few weeks, I have taken hundreds of phone calls from colleagues within the Dáil and Seanad, and from friends and acquaintances within the Party all around the country. That's routine for any TD, except that normally, those phone calls used to be about policies or local problems, about personal objectives, about national issues or regional concerns. These days, almost without exception, they are about personalities. Who had said what to which media? Who was the latest with a statement about vision? Who was drifting away from which block? What was the next scandal due to break and whose leadership prospects would be affected by it?

If this trend in the phone calls had happened directly after the vote of no confidence in November, it would be understandable, and there would be the hope that it would die away and we could get back to what we were put in Dáil Eireann to do: legislate for the future of Ireland and solve its present-day problems.

But three months after the no confidence motion, the pattern has now become standard. It is not a sudden fever, but a chronic ailment, in which gossip has displaced substantive issues and what is trivial has taken over from what is important. The camaraderie, trust and sense of common purpose which always distinguished Fianna Fail is disappearing as people concentrate, instead, on being in the know about who's in/ who's out, who's planning to cast their hat in the ring or hang onto their hat and their dark horse status. Members of what was, until relatively recently, a professional team committed to the good of the nation, are now looking over their shoulders, lying in wait for each other, and selling each other down the river for a positive mention in a newspaper. It's all hidden agenda stuff.

None of that adds up to the Fianna Fail Party I joined and I am still passionately loyal. The Fianna Fail Party I joined was:

● The party that would make us competitive with any other country in the world — but make sure that we retained the culture and tradition that made us different and special.

The party where you could depend on colleagues to be there when you needed them, even if they disagreed with you on particular issues; The party capable of pulling wide and complex interests into an achieved consensus, where disagreement was normal, but ridicule and personal caricature was not.

● The party that believed in potential, and celebrated success while always reaching out to individuals and groups who were less successful in a practical, unpatronising way.

● The party that listened, so that each and every public representative had an accurate picture of the concerns in his or her local area, to inform the overall policy-building within the party.

● The party of single party Government, or, if the worst came to the worst, of vigorous and relentless opposition.

● The party that got things done, in or out of Government.

Fianna Fail can be that party again — and more. But it urgently needs radical re-organisation. It needs to be re-financed. And it needs to be setting national ideals and direction; not bucketing from one damaging internal crisis to another.

Structural re-organisation is certainly needed by the party. The days of the cumann at every crossroads are long gone. Those were the days before the EC, the days before mass media, mass transmit and centralised schooling. Formal membership of political parties is reducing, not only here but in Britain and other countries. People today have many more options than they did in the past when it comes to expressing their views or influencing change. They don't have to join a political party. Fianna Fail must recognise this change in two ways. It must create structures which facilitate participation. It must also create links with people who may never formally join the party structure, but who could contribute to it and who could gain from some looser involvement.

A political party runs on shared ideals. But without enough money to run the operation, the engine seizes. The Fianna Fail engine has not yet seized for lack of finance, but the possibility is too close for comfort. Dropping totals from national collections, and even more pointedly the abysmal returns from large urban areas for those collectors, mean that the Party is desperately vulnerable. Without the money to run an election properly, the party is missing an essential planning and development tool. In future, state support for the democratic political institutions would seem to be a better option than the funding methods used up to now. State support would provide accountability and transparency, so that the public could have no worries that substantial political institutions could improperly influence legislation. But in advance of such a radical change, Fianna Fail must balance its own books and do it quickly.

Structural re-organisation and re-financing has to be matched by a clear strategic intent; a political plan understood and shared by the membership and communicated using the best modern media in the general public. Structured, solvent, and sending out a clear message — that's what we have to be.

The voter should be able to say, at any given time, what a particular political party stands for, what its priorities are, where it's heading towards — and we've failed to make the voter clear on any of these things in relation to FF for some time. Bluntly, other, smaller parties have been the ones to run with specific intent in a way that made sense to its populace, while Fianna Fail looked like a shapeless monolith.

This was very visible when we fought the '89 election. We fought it on track record. We fought it in retrospective claims: "see how well we've done, these last few years". We should have fought it saying "here's where Ireland must go, and here's how Fianna Fail plans to get us there." We should have fought it in the future tense. Instead, we fought it in self-congratulatory past tense and the electorate didn't join in the congratulations.

The electorate is never interested in the last performance of governments. The electorate wants to know what's on offer for the future. The electorate wants to vote for those who can spot and acknowledge problems and be relied on to tackle them.

If Fianna Fail is to have the appeal in the '90s that it did in earlier years then the party must have more than its time-honoured basic tenets. It must have contemporary objectives and be able to paint, for the public, a picture of the Ireland we should have in the year 2025.

Those contemporary objectives must include:

● A concerted and innovative drive to tackle unemployment. In addition, industrial policy must increasingly maximise cross-border co-operation, must reinforce existing links between public and private sector, and must release the potential of the information and services sectors.

● A series of initiatives to make Ireland the environmental oasis of Europe, where air, water and soil are so demonstrably pristine that all food products coming from this country would have an instantly obvious advantage throughout Europe.

● Bringing new creativity and energy to the promotion of our tourist product and to the creation of activity holidays to build upon Ireland's traditional attractions.

● Adjusting the codes to eliminate the poverty trap which sees some workers being paid less than they would get on welfare.

● Addressing the obstacles — actual and attitudinal — which are putting a 'glass ceiling' on the forward progress of women in our society.

Above all, Fianna Fail needs to show leadership in its interpretation of what a politician's job is. We are rapidly moving away from the politician-as-messenger years. Where we should be going is towards a model of the politician as a regional thinker on concepts affecting his or her own area, as a listener to individual and group concerns, as a driver of legislation which respects our traditions and values while making a progressive social impact. Public representatives ought to be able to refer to their professional work with pride, and to see themselves as both local ombudsmen (helping people cope with unresponsive administrative systems) and as policy catalysts.

In a sense, there couldn't be a better time to get this organisational renewal and national leadership going. The opposition, through a loss of identity, internal ideological battles and, in some instances, sheer poor performance, are giving us all the space we need. The space is there for substantive and courageous action to re-establish Fianna Fail as an organisation you can be proud to belong to, with a sense of mission which is sensitive to the radical changes in family and work life.

The space is there — but there's a closing date. We may get only one more chance to prove to the electorate that Fianna Fail should be in power as a single party government.

The space is there — but there's a price. That price includes a relinquishing of power at the top, done, in the best interests of the party, with dignity and speed.

If we don't make these changes, then we will still have a place, but it will be a sadly restricted place in Irish public life.

Either we develop an agenda we can all be proud of, or we get lost forever in the hidden agenda.

● *Leadership challengers and former Fianna Fail ministers Padraig Flynn (left) and Albert Reynolds: "Three months after the no-confidence motion ... the camaraderie, trust and sense of common purpose which always distinguished Fianna Fail is disappearing"*

SEND US YOUR TAX RETURN BY JAN 31

The Pádraig Flynn feature that led the *Sunday Tribune* to predict Haughey would not resign

Ard fheis – Taoiseach Albert Reynolds with advisor Tom Savage

Dublin Opinion's satirical take on Brian Lenihan Snr, who was always willing to do defensive media waffle when Haughey was under pressure

Giving Children Back Their Childhood

The Taoiseach's address to the nation on the IRA ceasefire last night.

THE PEOPLE who stand to gain most from yesterday's ceasefire probably don't know anything about it, and they probably aren't going to see this broadcast either. They are our children north and south, our children and our grandchildren.

They weren't around for the past 25 years of grief and tragedy. They don't know what a ceasefire can do. But they're not alone in that. None of us knows exactly what a complete cessation of violence can do.

The possibilities are so huge and so positive, and I know some of them, and I want to share those with you tonight.

The first thing I know is this. A complete ceasefire gives children back their rights, whether they're on the Falls or the Shankill, the Waterside or the Bogside. It gives them back their right to childhood.

That basic human right was stolen from generations of children in the North of Ireland by violence. Before they went to school they were used to the rituals of warfare. Their souls were tattooed with poisoned messages.

A ceasefire hands childhood back to the children, giving them the right to explore their world and discover unthreatening, simple things like water and sand and paints and uncomplicated friendship.

THERE are people watching tonight who have stood in the rain at peace rallies, listening to the speeches, praying for a result, holding flowers — and then going home, the hope ebbing out of them.

Some of the peacemakers have been working at it for more than two decades. Some started more recently when they saw a picture of a little boy with a baby on his knee, both of them orphaned by a bomb — or when they looked at a picture of a little girl, her two legs rigid in plaster, tubes everywhere, unconscious on a hospital bed. Peacemakers often became committed because of a desperate hurt to a child or to a family.

The complete ceasefire is a response to that commitment. It's a response many of the peacemakers thought might never happen. But it has happened.

No single person or group "owns" this ceasefire. It was earned, shaped and created by people who have suffered, people who have sympathised, people who have taken action to indicate that they wanted peace and would not settle for anything but peace.

Like everyone in this country, I had always wanted peace, I had always been willing to work for peace. In the days before I became leader of Fianna Fáil something happened that changed me from being someone willing to work for peace, to someone obsessed by peace. It was yet another atrocity.

Because of that, I put peace at the top of my agenda. I decided to have the courage of my simplicities: I wasn't going to get bogged down in the complex subtleties of myth or history.

DURING the past two years, I don't think I was ever in doubt about the progress we were making. Partly because I am a cronic optimist — but mainly because I knew that there were good people working constantly, working relentlessly, working with the patience and the passion you bring to the task that will define your life — make you proud to have lived.

The Tánaiste, Dick Spring, was a constant and significant presence. The two of us worked together with an uncompetitive serious trust that is rare between politicians of different parties.

John Hume also greatly contributed. Together we established a set of principles to address in a democratic spirit some of the key concerns of Northern Republicans.

But I will probably never be able to give public credit to many people who contributed immeasurably to this complete ceasefire. They have shown courage and patriotism, openness and resilience. Even when choosing to be anonymous, they have a right to be very proud of their achievement.

A COMPLETE ceasefire is a beginning, not an ultimatum or a threat. A ceasefire is not the continuation of a war by another means. It is the absence of war. It is an open door for decency, for normality — and for re-discovering each other as human beings, not as stereotypes and enemies.

Wartime reduces the marvellous complexity of individuals and their beliefs into a crude 'Us' and 'Them'. In peacetime, we don't have to be so narrowly defined. We can learn to value difference and the strength it gives. We can be informed by our history, but not confined by it.

A complete ceasefire isn't something passive either. Every individual on this island, every tradition now has a clear responsibility to show imagination and flexibility. The British Government has pledged to help the Irish people find agreement among themselves.

The Irish Government is absolutely committed to including everyone in political dialogue. We are committed to ensuring that every voice is heard — and listened to.

There is no reason for anyone to fear peace. In particular the Unionists, the other tradition on this island, have nothing to fear. This ceasefire hasn't happened because of some deal or hidden concession. I have been direct and unambiguous at all times throughout the years leading to this ceasefire and I am being direct and unambiguous now. There is no deal. There are no hidden agreements.

A process of dialogue and of persuasion within the tenets of democracy; that's all we're committed to, that's all we can hope for and work towards. But we must work towards it. And for that reason, I hope that Loyalist paramilitaries too

> 'Some of the peacemakers started working at it when they saw a picture of a little boy with a baby on his knee, both orphaned by a bomb.'

Pictured above are Darren Baird, 9, and his baby sister, Lauran Elizabeth, at their home shortly after their parents and sister were killed in Shankill bombing last October.

Albert Reynolds' ceasefire speech in the media, including the two orphaned children of whom he spoke

Bertie Ahern opens the new premises of the then Carr Communications

The Obama presidential visit where Albert Reynolds' dementia was sadly evident

Long after they didn't get to work together as Mary Harney wanted, she makes Terry an Honorary Doctor of Letters at University of Limerick

I met MGQ at the first training session we provided for Fianna Fáil and found her intimidating. She didn't necessarily set out to intimidate, but if intimidation was required, she was up for that. Tom adored her from the first day he met her, and the two of them were constantly in touch; he later became her adviser when she served as Minister for Justice under Albert Reynolds. In one odd way, he regularly stepped way out of line. Because he thought she looked great after she'd had a perm, he constantly nagged her, after she'd got rid of the curls, to go back to them. And she just as constantly told him to eff off.

Nobody ever got Máire to do anything she didn't want to do. Sitting in the Secretary's office in Fianna Fáil's HQ in Mount Street during one general election, I witnessed Fionnuala O'Kelly do a superb briefing arising from some election crisis (they always come thick and fast during any election). Someone in authority decided that MGQ needed to go on radio and TV and sort this out. O'Kelly agreed, but pointed out that several headquarters people had tried her every phone and the phones of everybody close to her. No response. Séamus Brennan muttered that he expected nothing less of MGQ during the run-up to an election. She would tell anybody who wanted her to leave the door-knocking even for a minute to get stuffed, but had long ago learned that simply not returning phone calls was even quicker than taking the time to tell people to get stuffed. On this occasion, nobody found her and someone else did the broadcast. Not as well as she'd have done it, but the Queen of the West wasn't for turning.

That dogged resolution was one of the MGQ characteristics that made me timorous in her presence. I steered clear of her, happy to see Tom escort her to events the two of them had to attend, but neither her husband, John Quinn (who lived and worked in Galway), nor I would be seen dead at.

Gradually, though, I came to appreciate why Tom thought she was so marvellous. She was a long-termer when it came to friendships, for example, which is always a good sign. She had a handful of girlfriends from school and college days who stayed friends with her throughout their lives, once telling a story about a bunch of them holidaying together in Switzerland when they were nineteen or twenty. Irish speakers, the lot of them, they gathered, before going down to dinner, on a balcony in the sunset, watching the 'talent' below them in the open-air restaurant and commenting aloud in Irish on how sexy or attractive each one was. In a pause, the group of them was stuck to the ground to hear a male voice from the balcony overhead speaking Irish.

'Isn't it shocking', the voice commented in excellent Connemara Irish, 'to hear young Irish women speaking in such crude terms of men they don't know.'

The girlfriends stared at each other in horror. That was all the voice said. The young women sneaked into the bedroom a couple of them shared, moving quietly as if quietness would make a difference to the strange situation. Should they go down to dinner or not? The decision was made to go down. They girded their loins, checked their hair and off they went. Seated, they looked around to see if they could identify the owner of the disapproving comment, but nobody looked familiar, so they got on with the meal and the glasses of wine and were well into the main course before the door onto the al fresco area opened and out stepped Joseph Cunnane, the Archbishop of Tuam, who immediately came right over to them and started to tease them about their earlier observations, much to their relief.

If Máire Geoghegan-Quinn had a bunch of close women friends from school and college days, she had also made friendships in politics with men like Noel Treacy, Charlie McCreevy and Brendan Daly. The men who liked Geoghegan-Quinn found her clever and fun. She had the courage of a lion, and a shyness that her political career meant she had to fight off every day. In common with Pádraig Flynn, she was not close to Mary O'Rourke, who Flynn referred to in private as 'a headless chicken' incapable of strategic thought, unlike Máire.

During the period when Fianna Fáil was in power in the late eighties, Máire Geoghegan-Quinn's position on Haughey began a relentless shift from positive to negative, so that when, in 1991, she was chosen to give the warm-up speech for her leader at the party's ard fheis, it put her between a rock and an extremely hard place. She sat down with Tom Savage and laid out the problem for him. She had to do the speech or resign two weeks before the ard fheis. If she resigned it would be seen as an egregiously vicious betrayal of a leader and of the collegial responsibility she bore him. But she was not prepared to deliver a load of complimentary clichés about a man in whom she no longer believed.

Tom called me in, explained the dilemma and indicated that I would need to write a great speech. I went and got a Dictaphone. When I came back, Tom left the two of us together and I started to record our conversation. When I was sure I had enough, I was also sure I knew how to write a speech so that, on first hearing, it would sound as encomiastic and celebratory as the usual twaddle delivered at such events, and that it would not be until days afterwards that the half-life of the speech would begin to be noticed.

As it turned out, it took longer than a few days for all but one auditor to make that deduction. RTÉ's Gerald Barry, writing in the *Sunday Tribune*, nailed what had happened: the speech had been celebratory, but it was cast in the past tense. It invited the audience to applaud the end of a reign. It was the equivalent of the statement famously put out by the British Home Office to the effect that 'the king's life is moving peacefully to its close.' And, above all, it was honest in a way such speeches don't tend to be – threaded through with the contradictions that had crumpled MGQ's regard for Haughey, and ending with a blunt statement:

> There will never be a time like it again: never such excitement, never such achievement, never such heartache, never such happiness, as the time they will talk of as the Haughey era.

Terry Keane, Haughey's mistress, later maintained that she had spotted what MGQ was at, but nobody else around him ever claimed that. For MGQ herself, however, the die was cast and within weeks she was telling Haughey that 'The people of Galway West never want to see your face on an election poster again.' Haughey's inner team became convinced that a slow-burn assassination was in the works, led by Albert Reynolds, who was still a Cabinet Minister, and involving members of the Country & Western Alliance.

Nothing could have been further from the truth. Albert believed he was seeing 'Haughey become more and more dictatorial', and he hated 'the series of shotgun elections that had caused instability within the party as well as the country'. Pádraig Flynn had eventually come round to believing what he had always thought was a myth: Haughey's relationship with Terry Keane. Flynn, a genuinely devout Catholic, found this offensive, particularly the realisation that the commentary on the affair that was charted in a marginally satirical column in the *Sunday Independent* was in fact largely true. Flynn hated the fact that Maureen Haughey had to absorb that weekly humiliation.

They met, did the Country & Western Alliance, and Tom met with them, but as a group they never identified a killer strategy, and whenever they came close to one it tended to be scuppered by some individual within Fianna Fáil's parliamentary party expressing the same doubts they had, but from an unattached and not always helpful angle. So, towards the end of 1991, Deputy Seán Power tabled a motion calling for the end of Mr Haughey's leadership. Albert, who, as we shall see, had a timeline in his head and was not privy to Power's move before he made it, was furious, seeing the move as premature. On the other hand, if Albert, known to be the leader of potential dissidents over in the West, refused to back Power's motion, this would put him in much the same position as the ard fheis speech had put Geoghegan-Quinn in, just weeks earlier.

At three in the morning, Tom and Albert sat in the elegant sitting room of Albert's Ailesbury Road apartment, cups of cooling tea between them, with Albert going round and round the possibilities open to him.

'Should I vote against Haughey?' he finally asked, as if the question had not been articulated earlier.

'Albert. If you don't vote against Haughey, there is no possibility that you will ever lead Fianna Fáil,' Tom told him. 'If you do vote against Haughey there is every possibility that you will never lead Fianna Fáil.'

Albert digested this and then summed it all up. 'They're not going to succeed,' he said, 'but I'm not going to be a hypocrite.'

Máire, Albert and P. Flynn voted against Haughey's continuation as leader. The motion was defeated by fifty-five votes to twenty-two. The Country & Western team had to resign from Cabinet, with MGQ, as soon as her car crossed the Shannon that night, passing one bonfire after another, each surrounded by a cheering group of people. But 1991 moved into 1992, and all that had been achieved was that the three were no longer in government, while Mr Haughey continued as leader and as Taoiseach.

P.J. Mara had always loathed us and was one of the factors ensuring that by the late eighties, we were doing less consulting with Haughey. This wasn't a problem – our non-political business was growing, particularly overseas. During this time, we provided training and consultancy in seventeen overseas locations. In addition, Tom was diagnosed with cancer, which took him out of commission for several months and was terrifying.

But the major factor creating distance between the Fianna Fáil leader and us was Mara, who constantly plotted to keep us away from Haughey. Once, when Haughey sent a group of backbenchers for basic media training, he told Tom that Mara would come to introduce the course. Knowing that Mara had just tried to replace us with a former staff member of ours who had gone out on his own (but had stayed good friends with us, and had let us know about this offer), I met PJ at the front door, brought him into a small office, and questioned him about him trying to replace us with others. He flustered and blustered. I also told him that leaking to *Phoenix* magazine, as he had, the likelihood of CJ firing us wasn't a great ploy, since it alerted Fianna Fáil's competition to the possibility of us coming off retainer and becoming available to them.

'Doesn't matter to me if you choose not to have an exclusive relationship with us,' I told him. 'Other political parties will hire us, no bother. I just don't want Mr Haughey to believe that you have reason to mistrust us, and I've no doubt that's what you'll tell him.'

The phone on the table between us rang, and I lifted it, ready to be cross with the receptionist for ignoring my instruction to hold all calls for the duration of the conversation with Mara, only to find Charles Haughey on the other end, wanting to talk with Mara.

'He's right here with me,' I said. 'We've just been discussing how important trust is'.

I handed over the phone and left the room. Mara literally never spoke another word to me and worked hard to ensure we had nothing to do with his leader from the mid-eighties onward, ending our connection with one of the most fascinating men we had ever trained or written for. As a visiting expert in communications, to work with him was to operate in a bubble of distant intimacy akin to being the music teacher to a monarch who loved music: you achieved a transient connection, a shared pleasure in the task, uncomplicated by expectations of favours.

It also allowed you to wonder, from a distance, at how a man could so misdirect his genius. Tom once remarked that Haughey always came in a side window, even when the front door was open, such was his visceral need for conspiracy, to be cleverer than the context. In his early days as a minister, CJ was exceptionally productive, creating legislation that was innovative and effective. He knew what he was doing back in the early sixties. He was an able and impressive parliamentarian. Even the then leader of the opposition, Fine Gael's James Dillon, described the young Haughey as being possessed of 'extraordinary and exceptional ability' as well as 'extraordinary erudition'. What turned him towards failure to use that erudition and ability on behalf of Fianna Fáil and the nation and instead go for crookedness and conspiracy is a mystery.

In which context, Tom always used a quotation from *A Man for All Seasons* to underpin the dangers of personal ruthlessness, even when it was, in the case of the play's character, hypothetically deployed for a good cause. In the play Thomas More's intemperate son-in-law to be, William Roper, says he would cut down every law in England if he had to, in pursuit of the devil. 'This country is planted thick with laws from coast to coast, man's laws, not God's laws,' More tells Roper. 'And if you cut them down (and you're just the man to do it) do you really think you could stand upright in the winds that would blow then?'

Tom always carried that quotation in his wallet, handwritten on a scrappy folded-up bit of paper, because he believed it to crystallise such an important principle. It was a principle Haughey never grasped. He spent his life ignoring the laws – written and unwritten – on which this country operates, confident that he would never find himself on an open plain trying to withstand the winds blowing unimpeded at him.

The fatal gale, of course, came in the form of Roscommon's Seán Doherty.

10

THE WOMAN WHO MADE SEÁN DOHERTY TELL THE TRUTH

Around that time, if Seán Doherty's name was mentioned, it summoned up for me a black and white picture of a man looking slightly stuffed in his stiff formality. That was because I knew of Doherty only through Peter Murtagh and Joe Joyce's book *The Boss*, a masterful portrayal of Charles Haughey, in which there were a number of pictures of the man. The two journalists gave the impression that Doherty was 60 per cent wide boy, 20 per cent former garda and 20 per cent faithful acolyte of Mr Haughey, and so I was taken aback, mid-morning on 21 January 1992, a Tuesday, when Tom said Seán Doherty would be in the office in half an hour, and that I'd have to deal with him, since Tom was chairing a meeting of the Retirement Planning Council of Ireland, of which he was a founder.

'Why? What does he want?'
'Don't know. Brian Lenihan rang and asked if we'd see him.'
'And you said yes, knowing you wouldn't be here? Thanks a bunch.'
'It's probably about the *Nighthawks* gaffe.'
'Tom, I've never seen frigging *Nighthawks*, I know Doherty only by repute and you could get out of that meeting.'

He shook his head.

'This is going to be like the sheep rustling,' I said. The night before, we'd had a bloody fine row about whether or not sheep rustling in the border counties was unethical. I said it was. Tom said I was suburban Dublin and had no clue about real life north of the Pale. I told him ethics were immutable, with or without county boundaries. He said sheep were stupid, anyway, and that he couldn't stick them. Cows were annoying, fair enough, but sheep were too stupid to live. I said the issue was sheep rustling, not him disliking sheep because they were thick as planks, and he demanded that I define what sheep rustling was and of course I couldn't precisely say, so he recommended I not get so effing high-minded about something before I knew what the hell it was. And now he was dumping the moral equivalent of a sheep rustler on me. I indicated I took a dim view. He hugged me round the shoulders, ignoring my view, dim or otherwise, and disappeared, scattering gravel from his car wheels against the wall of the old railway station in Taney Road, Dundrum.

After Tom had gone, it struck me that a newspaper I had recently thrown out had something about Doherty in it. That newspaper was the *Sunday Tribune*, edited by Vincent Browne, who, the previous week, had invited Pádraig Flynn to write a substantial piece about the future of Fianna Fáil, which had necessitated me attending on Flynn in his now small office (small because he was no longer a minister) with a tape recorder to get the material from the horse's mouth.

'Why does Vincent want this?' I asked, pushing the tape recorder into the middle of the big table. Pádraig always insisted that if a woman was on her own in the room with him, she was on the other side of the big table. He would not let you come to his side, even if you wanted to show him the details of a document. In a political world where the hand up the skirt was a commonality and a cliché, this was refreshing, if occasionally awkward. On this occasion, his shrug suggested that (a) he didn't know, (b) he didn't care, (c) Vincent was Vincent and barking anyway, so why was it worth speculation?

'Has to be a news peg I'm missing,' I said, before interviewing him. I had no clue, as would become apparent later, just how large that news peg was. As Pádraig started to talk he surprised me by his prophetic – and, as it turned out, accurate – negativity. 'If something isn't done and done quickly, then the most influential and representative political party in the history of the state will be crucially weakened,' he said. 'Fianna Fáil is heading for a century in which the party will get steadily smaller and poorer. Young Fianna Fáil members will face years of opposition or of coalition.'

As far as he was concerned, coalition was probably worse than opposition. He believed that going into coalition, as Haughey had done with the Progressive Democrats, was a breach of what he loved to call Fianna Fáil's 'core values'. It didn't help that his minister of state in the department was Mary Harney, who loathed him almost as much as he loathed her and frequently persuaded Haughey to slap Flynn down when the two of them crossed swords. But, as the tape recorder ran, Flynn talked about more than coalition. He talked about the camaraderie and sense of common purpose, which he believed had always distinguished Fianna Fáil, disappearing as people concentrated instead on being in the know about who was 'in' with the leader and who was 'out', as well as who might be planning to cast their hat into the ring or hang on to their hat *and* their dark horse status.

> Members of what was, until relatively recently, a professional team committed to the good of the nation are now looking over their shoulders, lying in wait for each other and selling each other down the river for a positive mention in a newspaper. None of that adds up to the Fianna Fáil party I joined and to which I am still passionately loyal. The Fianna Fáil party I joined was the party that would make us competitive with any other country in the world – but make sure that we retained the culture and tradition that made us different and special. The party where you could depend on colleagues to be there when you needed them, even if they disagreed with you on particular issues; the party

capable of pulling wide and complex interests into an achieved consensus, where disagreement was normal, but ridicule and personal caricature was not.

He was pointing out that people had more options, more things to be doing with their personal time than joining a political party, and so structures were needed to make participation easier and more intriguing.

The voter should be able to say, at any given time, what a particular political party stands for, what its priorities are, where it's leading towards – and we've failed to make the voter clear on any of those things in relation to Fianna Fáil for some time. Bluntly, other, smaller parties have been the ones to run with specific issues that made sense to the populace while Fianna Fáil looked like a shapeless monolith. We need a series of initiatives to make Ireland the environmental oasis of Europe, where air, water and soil are so demonstrably pristine that all food products coming from this country would have an instantly obvious advantage throughout Europe. We are rapidly moving away from the politician-as-messenger years. Where we should be going is towards a model of the politician as a regional thinker on concepts affecting his or her own area, as a listener to individual and group concerns, as a driver of legislation which respects our traditions and values while making a progressive social impact. Public representatives ought to be able to refer to their profession with pride, and to see themselves as both local ombudsmen (helping people cope with unresponsive administrative systems) and as policy catalysts.

I asked him what would happen if none of what he was calling for transpired.
'If we don't make these changes, then we will still have a place, but it will be a sadly restricted place in Irish public life.'

I transcribed Pádraig's words, edited them into a draft, faxed it to him, dealt with his changes, faxed a fair copy to him and he sent it off to Vincent Browne, who later telephoned Pádraig with a couple of extra questions, one of which elicited the statement from Flynn that Haughey had no intention of resigning or retiring in the short or medium term. That quote put a shot of the former minister on the front page.

The day Tom dumped Seán Doherty in my lap, I retrieved that newspaper from a black plastic rubbish sack to see what else was in it, knowing – because I was familiar with it – that none of Pádraig's column offered any insight into why Doherty would be looking for our help, but figuring something else in the paper might advance my knowledge of the Doherty-authorised bugging of the phones of journalists Bruce Arnold and Geraldine Kennedy in the 1980s, which had happened on Haughey's watch but without his authorisation or knowledge, according to his own statements on the issue.

The paper, within a full-page analysis by Diarmuid Doyle, carried a quotation from John Waters' book *Jiving at the Crossroads*:

> Throughout the seventies and early eighties ... the denizens of Dublin 4 ... had invested all their impatience, their embarrassment, their righteous resentment, in the figure of Charles Haughey. Now, in the late eighties, nearly twenty years after the Arms Crisis, they found that Haughey was the only one willing and able to do their dirty work, to knock the national economy into shape after the failure of their hero Garret FitzGerald. They needed Haughey for the moment, and Haughey could not achieve power without their support. But they also needed the lightning conductor, which Doherty provided, to take their feelings of impatience, embarrassment and resentment back safely to earth, to allow them to rationalise what they could never openly admit. And so Haughey strode in to the light, while Doherty brooded under the shadow of the flawed pedigree cloud ... it was not enough to record that Doherty had made mistakes and

that he had been overzealous in his loyalty to both his leader and his people, that he was the kind of political cat from whose claws the cream of power might have been more prudently protected. All that he stood for, and all who stood by him, had to be stamped out.

In that copy of the newspaper, analyst Diarmuid Doyle stated that John Waters saw former Justice Minister Seán Doherty as:

> an unfairly maligned politician, caught in the grip of a fundamental debate about Irish politics – between an urban, liberal Dublin 4 attitude to life, and a rural, conservative, traditional outlook. Waters's comments in the book, often a strenuous defence of Doherty and his supporters, are at odds with what most of the Senator's colleagues in the Senate and Fianna Fáil feel about him. Many cannot conceal their distaste for a man who was at the centre of the GUBU period of 1982 and whose comments on *Nighthawks* on RTÉ on Wednesday about the phone tapping of journalists' phones had returned him once again to the centre of the political stage.

Those comments seemed to imply that Mr Haughey had known all about the phone tapping at the time it happened. Just why Doherty would have chosen this time to revive an old controversy wasn't clear, but he seemed to have had an unproductive meeting before Christmas with a successor as Minister for Justice, Ray Burke. A storm of attributed motivations emerged after the Wednesday night *Nighthawks*. Some suggested it was cheap profile-raising, some that it was a 'ham-fisted' attempt to support Albert Reynolds, who had quietly told friends that any association with Doherty could only do damage to his slowly building campaign for the leadership of Fianna Fáil. One particularly convoluted theory was that Doherty had done it because he was secretly a member of Mary O'Rourke's team and was setting out to smear Reynolds. Another theory was that Doherty was 'well tore' on the night. He wasn't – he had not consumed alcohol at all before going on the programme.

Whatever way you looked at it, it was a mess, and when Doherty got talking, after he and his wife were shown to a smallish meeting room and supplied with coffee, it looked like an even worse mess. Maura Doherty sat mute while her husband talked about the *Nighthawks* programme and the feeding frenzy provoked by the comments he had made. Neither of us pointed out that he had, in the first heady moments after the programme was in the can, actively nudged the presenter, Shay Healy, into paying more attention to the comments than the presenter was ever likely to on his own.

Doherty, who was so pale I wondered if he was always possessed of such pallor or wasn't well, said he had told Shay Healy on air that Haughey knew about the bugging at the time, and this comment was causing him untold difficulty. He had gone to Brian Lenihan Sr with the problem, and Lenihan had told him that he should come to Carr Communications because we would 'put a formula of words around it'. With that, he drank half his cup of tea. Maura Doherty looked at me without raising her head: go on, let's see what the spin doctor has to offer.

'Let me get this right.' I said slowly. 'You said something unwise on live TV, right?'

Right, he nodded.

'Was it true or false, what you said?'

True, he said, looking irritated by all this palaver.

'If what you said on the programme was the truth, the only "formula of words" that'll get you out of it is a lie,' I said, offended by the assumption that we would help him craft the lie, and even more offended knowing that a refusal would make us seem naive, po-faced or both.

He was nonplussed, not least because we were in a room so small, it nearly required a vote to be taken to decide which of the three of us should stalk out first. Because of Maura Doherty, none of us stalked out. She cut through the 'formula of words' stuff and issued an ultimatum. He was going to tell the truth, starting now. He had taken enough grief, done enough covering up.

'You've been the fall guy long enough,' she told him, steely with sustained bitterness. 'You've suffered plenty and so have all your family.'

At the mention of his daughters, who had grown from childhood through adolescence in the nine years during which their father's name had been synonymous with abuse of power and the squalid invasion of privacy, Doherty wept.

'You owe it to us and you owe it to yourself', Maura Doherty finished, ignoring the tears, 'to tell the truth now.'

He shook his head the way a dog coming out of water does and began to talk. He was like a man trying to learn what he believed in by hearing himself say it aloud. He talked about how honesty sometimes wasn't a virtue, or at least not the ultimate virtue. The ultimate virtue might be fidelity to what you believed, loyalty to the people you believed in. It was easy, he said, to think of morality as black and white, but it wasn't; it was complicated by families and friendships, teams and townlands, colleagues and political parties. His wife watched him, still as a stone, intent. I asked him questions – not many – about the phone tapping and why it had happened. He counted the sequence off on his fingers. First, the cabinet was leaking like a sieve, to the detriment of good governance. Second, as Minister for Justice, it was his job to investigate those leaks.

What struck me, listening to Seán Doherty, was that he wasn't – up to this point – trying to justify himself to me or indeed to himself. He passionately believed that he had an obligation to fulfil and he had fulfilled it by tapping the two phones. He was convinced that he must establish (as he had earlier said to a journalist):

> … who was taking information out of the most important boardroom in the country and making it available without authority to the national media and to others and I felt that that was wrong. So did my colleagues in cabinet feel that it was wrong

and consequently I was required to ensure that that would be stopped and I consulted with the authorities at that time and one of the methods that was decided upon was the tapping of telephones, and anybody else that says otherwise or tries to abandon himself or herself from that situation is not telling the truth.

That's what he had said earlier, and he said a version of it to me, now. As far back as 1983, Doherty had acknowledged instigating discussions with An Garda Síochána and the Department of Justice into the possibility of tapping journalists' phones as a way of finding out who around the cabinet table was providing them with what he regarded as confidential discussions. Now, he was telling me that while he had taken the initiative, he had *not* come up with the idea. I stayed silent and he started to talk about process, about signing official Garda warrants to authorise the activity. It was clear that, as a former garda himself, he was more comfortable with that process and with official signed documents, although, in this instance, where the initiative had come from was clearly more relevant than either.

'Finally', he said, coming to the end of the bit he felt reasonably at home with, 'finally …' He baulked and went silent.

'Finally …?' I prompted.

'I showed the Taoiseach the transcripts.'

I decided to leave to one side the issue of who had set him on this course of action and just stick with where he was in the narrative, pointing out that this was not what the Taoiseach had said when Fine Gael's Michael Noonan had revealed the phone tapping. Charlie Haughey had swiftly condemned it as 'an abuse of power' and had flatly stated that he would never 'have countenanced such action'. Far from seeing the transcripts, as Doherty was now claiming, Haughey maintained that he had been ignorant of the tapping while it was in progress. At no point in the venture had he been privy to what was going on. Back then, Doherty had confirmed what Charles Haughey said. And yes, he now affirmed, he had taken personal responsibility for the phone tapping.

'I had to support the Taoiseach's position. I was under enormous pressure,' he told me.

'But now you're saying he authorised the phone tapping.'

He shook his head and told me that I didn't understand Haughey. I didn't understand how someone like Haughey operated. Haughey didn't have to give anyone instructions. If you knew him, you incorporated his thinking into your own, so that when he gave the mildest hint, you knew what to do without coming back and annoying him asking for formal permission. Haughey had never, accordingly, formally authorised the taps, nor had he been asked to. Instead, he had created a context in which a loyal servant like Doherty would instigate them and keep the leader in the loop about what was going on. Shortly after taking over as minister, the context thus set, Doherty started to talk about cabinet and other high-level leaks with Joe Ainsworth, then assistant Garda commissioner. Ainsworth was in charge of An Garda Síochána's intelligence and security branch. At some early point – it wasn't clear precisely when – Mr Haughey had participated in a three-cornered meeting about leaks with Ainsworth and Doherty, having previously had discussions with both men about the issue. He was fully briefed, in other words, but, significantly, made no decision.

It was Doherty who began by ordering the tapping of the phone of Bruce and Mavis Arnold. Bruce wrote for the *Irish Independent*. It was Doherty who later ordered the tapping of the phone of *Sunday Tribune* reporter Geraldine Kennedy. Officials in the Department of Justice did not like any of this when it was first mooted and said the bugging shouldn't happen. Doherty ignored the advice of his own officials and signed the relevant documentation. He was now saying that Haughey knew about all this from day one, and that Doherty had kept him in the loop, including delivering him transcripts as the phone taps began to bear fruit. During the months during which the recordings of Vincent Browne, Geraldine Kennedy and Bruce Arnold had been going on, Mr Haughey had regularly received copies of transcripts of the more interesting conversations directly from Doherty's hands. He had read them. He had kept some of them, returning them long afterwards, returning some not at all. Yet, when the scandal broke, it was Doherty who took the blame and who, as a consequence, lost the front-bench post that meant so much to him.

I waited for him to talk bitterly about betrayal, but this was a well-trained foot soldier who knew how to go back to being a foot soldier if that was what the leader required. When his focus narrowed to personal grievance, he might make dark threats, but Doherty was fascinated by, and fascinating about, the bigger picture. He mused about the ambivalence of leadership, the fact that leadership might actually be defined by the capacity to sacrifice your own loyalists. He articulated how the needs of a political party might require one of its members to accept public excoriation as a liar, if that allowed the man at the top to continue as leader. Especially if the man at the top was Charles Haughey, with all his enmeshing genius, his overarching vision anchored – as Doherty saw it – in an unequalled appreciation of the down-and-dirty daily realities of politics.

He talked like a research scholar, rather than a country Dáil deputy. He talked like a man used to talking himself out of problems. He talked like a man building a ditch to keep out a rising tide – an irrevocably rising tide – that would swamp him the following day, when having achieved something of a career revival as Cathaoirleach of the Seanad, he would have to make a speech revisiting the horrors of nine years previously – and all as a result of his truth leakage on *Nighthawks*.

'All the old controversies will be revived,' he said, so softly I had to lean forward to hear him. 'I've served my sentence and now I'm going to be tried twice for the same offence and put my family, my constituents and the party through it all over again.'

The factor that had provoked his boomerang input on *Nighthawks* was the insistence of the Progressive Democrat partners in government that a bill incorporating phone-tapping elements be taken to the Houses of the Oireachtas at a time, as Doherty put it, 'when it could only deliver maximum embarrassment to me as Cathaoirleach of the Seanad'.

He was weeping again, the heels of his hands rammed against his eyes as if sheer force would stop the tears at the prospect of those he needed to love and admire him hearing, all over again, how he was a worthless, lying law-breaker, a former garda without the basic standards inculcated in members of the force, a wide boy personifying the quintessence of the old, 'fixer' Fianna Fáil.

But there was party outrage there too, outrage at a Fianna Fáil leader so malleable (as Doherty saw it) in the hands of a smaller party ('of renegades, let us never forget that, of renegades') as to be willing to force an endlessly obedient man to step up to the loyalty line, swallowing his pride and scattering the shards of integrity he had gathered around himself. Again. Nine years after the first time.

Maura Doherty never touched her husband. He wept alone, and when he wept, she looked at the table, sometimes scooping biscuit crumbs together and tipping them into an ashtray. Until it was time to monosyllabically push him to the next part of his story, and to the inevitability of where that story was taking him. Her very harshness, I began to realise, was stirring to life within him unresolved remnants of personal pride, strengthening his need to measure up to what he wanted his daughters to believe him to be.

When I left them in the clammy little room to try to make sense of the notes I had taken, it wasn't so much that a decision to go public had been taken as that both of them had acquiesced to an unspoken emerging inevitability. Asking a staff member to bring the two of them lunch, I disappeared into my office and started to type everything he had said. Then I cut about 90 per cent of what I had typed. Out went Doherty's statements that sometimes truth was a betrayal without merit, a betrayal that didn't serve the public good in any real way, but that could be endlessly destructive of values and culture and of an individual who, in himself, could make inestimable contributions to the nation.

People from our public relations division poked their heads around my office door, eyebrows raised.

'We might have to do a thing for tonight's television news,' I said and they said good luck with that. I stopped them as they headed out and asked what they meant.

'Of course, you don't watch television. There's a strike. RTÉ is on strike.'

'Hang on a second. How can they be on strike? I heard the radio this morning. I mean, I heard the news bulletin.'

'Yep, management are putting stuff on the air. It's all re-runs except the news. Guys that used to be newsreaders are reading the news. But there are no guests in studio because nobody's willing to pass the picket at the front gate on Nutley Lane.'

Someone pushed past the head of PR to give me a cup of coffee, then stayed to work out why I was sitting, opening and closing my mouth like a goldfish. Then a clumsy linked thought occurred to me. The Dohertys were actually sitting in a room that doubled as our video edit suite. I was a video editor. If I worked for RTÉ, I wouldn't be video-editing during a strike. Ergo, if Doherty was recorded somewhere other than in the RTÉ studios, RTÉ would be hard put to edit it. I said all this out loud, and the coffee-bearer smiled.

'Plus, they won't have anyone to contradict whatever he says,' I murmured.

'Sorry?'

'Well, P.J. Mara's hardly going to pass a picket.'

I suddenly realised that, if I timed it right, RTÉ would *have* to film it because the former reporters, now managers, would immediately know just how big a story it would be. Having filmed it, they might – probably would – have no choice but to put it out on the airwaves in its entirety. No mediation, no mitigation, no interpretation. Just the truth of this man speaking. That might solve one of the problems, which was that if Doherty was asked even one question, he would not be able to answer it, so exhausted and distraught was he by that point in the afternoon.

I printed off two copies of the script and handed one to one of the PR staff, asking her to deliver it to the Dohertys and hammer home to them that they had to be copper-bottomed guaranteed certain of every single statement therein. Then I asked the PR executive the name of the hotel nearest to RTÉ. The Montrose, she answered. Of course, I said. Okay, would she check if they would have a conference room we could book for about eight-thirty that evening? She shook her head.

'Eight o'clock,' she said. 'The journalists will need to be brought in first. Plus, RTÉ will need to set up and put up their lights. Even if the script is only ten minutes long, they then have to get it back to RTÉ and process it.'

I nodded and she went off to check, coming back within minutes to say it was possible, but they'd need a credit card. Ask Mr Doherty for his, I said, and she nodded. Doherty was not a retained client. She got the card, booked the room and suggested that a note go to newsrooms from Doherty's phone to invite them to send a reporter to an urgent press briefing.

'Hold it,' I said. 'Don't do anything yet. If we're sure we're doing it, then issue the invitation at seven-thirty.'

'Very tight,' she said disapprovingly.

I looked at her. She looked at me. Then she laughed. 'Very tight for a normal press briefing,' she amended, realising that no editor was going to be pompous about short notice on a story as big as this one was going to be.

I rejoined the Dohertys, to find, oddly, a copy of my book *Write and Get Paid for It* on the table between them. Obviously one of them had taken it down from the shelves behind them. Doherty said his wife wanted to write a book. I told her she was welcome to the paperback and to come back to me if I could help. However, right now, were they sure – swear-on-the-Bible sure – that there was nothing in the script that wasn't the truth? Yes, they said, they were sure.

'Right,' I said to him. 'Read it aloud.'

He started hesitantly and got worse, even though the script was in large type, was composed of short sentences and very much in the spoken word. Several times he halted and just looked at the pages in silence. When he reached the first reference to Haughey, he came adrift, crying at the prospect of being parted for ever from a man he believed to be the best leader Fianna Fáil ever had. On the one hand, Haughey had made it clear that he wanted the bugging done, had known everything about the phone tapping and had read the transcripts. On the other hand, he had later lied about all that in a way that left him alone in his culpability. Haughey had watched a man obeying unstated orders and in the process becoming a figure of national disrepute (or at least adding to an already poor reputation) and had never sought to help him, publicly or privately. And yet. And yet Doherty still adored him and agonised over the possibility of telling a damning truth about him. I have another John O'Connell here, I thought. A man who needs a hero. A man who needs to be bullied and demeaned and concurrently to be in a conspiracy of laughter, denigration of enemies and sneaky backroom stuff. Now, telling his own truth required him to betray the figure at the centre of all that, the leader he loved and admired.

Just as I expected him to pick up the reading of the script, he suddenly stood up and left the room. Maura Doherty said nothing. I checked the script to make sure I hadn't inadvertently included some verbal obstacle that was throwing him off. The door opened, and Doherty reappeared, his arms full of civil-service-type pale green folders, the kind that have a string through a hole at the top keeping the contents from falling out. He banged the load of them onto the table and started rifling through them. I pulled one of them over to my side of the table and opened it. It was the transcript of a conversation between George Colley and a journalist, I think Vincent Browne. Doherty came over to where he could read it and pointed at it.

'D'you see? D'you see? *That's* a leak from cabinet. There's another. *That's* what was going on. I told you. That's unconstitutional. Colley is a traitor.'

Maura Doherty asked tiredly why he had brought in all the folders, and he pulled three of them open at points where the top corner of pages was turned down. Those were among the transcripts Haughey had read, he told me. Trying to read the first of them, I found it was a gossipy conversation about the Mirabeau restaurant in Sandycove, a favourite Haughey/Terry Keane hangout. Doherty said those were the transcripts Haughey preferred. The ones about people having affairs and stuff. Maura Doherty reached over, took the open file from me, put it neatly in a pile with the others and did a 'Next item?' gesture at me.

It was now six o'clock. I told Doherty that if he was going to get this over with tonight, he had to be able to read the statement aloud without stopping. I explained the RTÉ situation and nodded at him to start again. This time he got through it. Just about. I turned the pages back and asked him to do it again. He did. His voice was shaky, particularly when he asked his own rhetorical question, 'Why should anybody believe Seán Doherty now, when he said something different nine years ago?'

> The answer to that is painfully obvious. I have nothing to gain by saying what I'm saying. Nothing to gain. Everything to lose. I'm resigning my post. You only do that for the truth. The bottom line is this: I have to live with me. I have a wife, I have four daughters, good friends, constituents, who have stood by me through a difficult decade. For my sake and for their sake, I'm saying 'Enough is enough'.

He read it and re-read it twice more. Agonised by what he was saying about Charles Haughey, palpably relieved to have the confirmation of it in front of him, as if he hadn't know the fullness of his own experience until it had been fed back to him in print.

One of our PR people knocked and opened the door, pointing at her watch. Doherty said he would visit the Gents and then head for the Montrose Hotel.

'Look, he may lose it,' I said to Maura Doherty in his absence. 'That means you must sit beside him and watch the script while he's talking, so you know exactly where he is in it at any point. If he dries up or cries, take the script from him and read it. You don't have to read it to camera. You don't have to have style. Just read it out loud.' She said 'Okay', and they went off, one of my staff with them.

I turned off the lights, locked up the building, took a copy of the script with me and went home. As my headlights filled the room directly inside the front door through the big windows of our Sutton house, Tom, lying on the couch watching sport, waved a casual back-handed welcome and got up to hug me at the door.

'Thanks a whole lot for dropping that on me.'

'Oh yeah, what happened?' he asked, putting on the kettle and turning down the TV.

'Around about now', I said, handing him the script, 'Doherty is going to start reading this to journalists and RTÉ cameras in the Montrose.'

I went down the corridor to the bedroom to change out of my suit and when I came back, Tom was leaning, two-handed, on the kitchen counter, the script in front of him, shaking his head.

'What?'

'Tess, this is going to bring down Haughey.'

'Ah bullshit, Tom. I mean, I've heard "this is going to bring down Haughey" so many times. You've said it often: he sees a request for resignation as an invitation to battle. Alert the troops, create an enemy. Attack them. Resignation never happens, and it's not going to happen now, either.'

'No, Tess, trust me. This will bring down Mr Haughey. I need to ring Albert Reynolds.'

Because the ground floor of the house was pretty much open plan, I could hear, if not all the words of the conversation, certainly its tone, which went, on Tom's part, from calm civility to infuriated impatience, which surprised me, because Tom had been working with the Country & Western Alliance of Albert, Máire Geoghegan-Quinn, Pádraig Flynn, Noel Treacy and (although based nearer Dublin) Charlie McCreevy with a view to Albert succeeding Haughey when the time came. If the time ever came. I had never heard Tom say a negative word about Reynolds, but the one-sided bit of this telephone conversation demonstrated Tom being seriously annoyed. Annoyed enough to raise his voice from its normal velvety near-whisper.

'No, Albert, no, there is nothing I can do about it,' I could hear him say. 'This balloon is going up and there's no stopping it. I just rang out of courtesy to give you a heads-up, okay?'

He disconnected the phone with untypical vehemence.

'What the hell was that about?' I asked, sitting down with a cup of tea in the TV room.

'He wants it stopped.'

'He wants *what* stopped?'

'Doherty. He seems to have some other plan* and he thinks Doherty is going to wreck it.'

It was now ten to nine. Tom rang Máire Geoghegan-Quinn and told her, not just what was happening, but about Albert's strangely hostile reaction. She couldn't make any sense of that but said she would let Noel Treacy and Charlie McCreevy know. I rang Pádraig Flynn, explained why and handed the phone over to Tom so he could tell Flynn about Albert wanting the whole thing aborted. Flynn clarified a couple of points, then thanked us and rang off.

At this stage it was about three minutes to the bulletin, which was opened by Kevin Healy, then a top manager in RTÉ after decades in the newsroom alongside luminaries like Gerry Barry. Doherty was the top story and after a brief scene-setter, they cut to the Montrose Hotel footage and a two-shot of Doherty and his wife. Although one of our staff had done rudimentary make-up on him so he wouldn't shine under the lights, he still looked grey with exhaustion. He began

---

* Dr Justin O'Brien, in his book about Haughey entitled *The Modern Prince*, stated that 'Albert Reynolds does not dispute the inevitable inference that he had some undertaking in advance of that confession that Haughey would go on an agreed date, and feared that the undertaking would be unravelled by Doherty's unexpected move. Reynolds confirms the plan involved "to some degree, shall we say", Dr John O'Connell, a former confidant of Haughey's.' O'Brien further records Albert, at the time when O'Brien contacted him, refusing to elaborate on the details of that plan, remarking mischievously that 'it may never be known.'

to read, his wife beside him rigid with the fear of having to take over if he could not continue.

'I am confirming tonight that the Taoiseach, Mr Haughey, was fully aware in 1982 that two journalists' phones were being tapped, and that he at no stage expressed a reservation about this action,' he said.

He went on to state that phone tapping had never been discussed at cabinet (thus confirming what Pádraig Flynn had told the *Sunday Tribune* the previous Sunday) and that he, Doherty, had never told the cabinet he was doing it. However, he went on, he had brought transcripts of the tapped phone calls to Mr Haughey and left them with him.

'I understand that the Taoiseach has already denied that this happened,' he continued, 'so I wish to reiterate it in specific terms. Each and every one of those relevant transcripts was transported by me to Mr Haughey's office and handed to him directly.'

Tom was making notes as he watched, his highly legible cursive lashing across a ruled A4 page. Doherty mentioned Haughey commenting, as soon as the tapping had been revealed, that he would never have countenanced such an abuse of power, and talked about why he had gone along, at the time, with a position he knew to be false.

'When I was later interviewed, I felt pressured to support Mr Haughey's stated position.'

When Doherty was about halfway through, Tom predicted that RTÉ was going to play the piece in its entirety. 'Is he going to take questions?'

I shook my head. I had briefed the two Dohertys on how to get out of the room quickly, and our PR staff had rehearsed it with them when they got to the Montrose Hotel.

Doherty read doggedly to the end, and the moment he finished, our phone started to ring. Knowing it wasn't going to be for me, I headed for bed while the Country & Western Alliance and dozens of other politicians and media people thrashed out with Tom what had happened.

The fight back began immediately after the broadcast, starting with a condemnatory statement from P.J. Mara. Around ten the following morning, a newspaper journalist rang to ask what my role had been. I laughed and asked him why he thought I might have had anything to do with it. It turned out that he had wandered around the car park of the Montrose until he found the Roscommon-registered car owned by the Dohertys and had spotted a copy of *Write and Get Paid for It* on the shelf inside the back window. When I came off the phone and told Tom, he smiled sadly at Maura Doherty being so tired and fearful that she had accidentally created such a distraction.

Charles Haughey moved quickly to rubbish everything that Doherty had said, oddly picking the Montrose Hotel as the venue for his own press conference. He did it completely on his own, sitting at the middle of a long table, with P.J. Mara standing in a corner. He was calm, authoritative and sure-footed.

'Told you it wouldn't bring him down,' I said to Tom.

'You just wait,' he said.

One of the papers the following day carried a series of close-up photographs of a paper clip Mr Haughey had fiddled with and destroyed during the press conference. Great shots, but symbolic only, I believed, of the inevitable tension Haughey had been under.

The intervention that shifted everything came from Haughey's former Fianna Fáil colleague, Des O'Malley, now head of the Progressive Democrats, then in coalition with Fianna Fáil. O'Malley described Doherty's confession (as it was now being called) as 'chilling'. That was the first staking out of the ground, and within days it was clear that Haughey's time at the top of Fianna Fáil was over, thanks to one of his erstwhile loyalists.

Later, the conspiracy theorists would go to work, spinning a web of intrigue, peopling the web with plotters and deciding that one woman – me – was responsible. They were right in only one regard. One woman *was* responsible. But that woman was Seán Doherty's wife, a clever, relentless woman who couldn't be persuaded by his fountain of words, who saw through his slapped-together certainties and who refused to be seduced by his capacity to amuse. A woman who knew the mechanics and the miseries of politics, but who was also a gifted teacher and writer. A woman who knew Doherty for what he was and was never going to let him get away with being anything less than he could be.

11

Haughey's Successor

One week after Seán Doherty's confession, on 30 January 1992 Charles Haughey told a Fianna Fáil parliamentary party meeting that he was stepping down from the leadership. The race was on to succeed him. The new leader would have to be ratified by the Dáil on 11 February. Despite Albert Reynolds' fears, expressed to Tom in forceful terms, that the confession would do him harm and must be stopped, and although Haughey had suggested the confession was all part of a plot on the part of Albert's supporters, it was obvious, within hours of Haughey announcing that he was going, that Albert – unless he made some astonishing mis-step – would win the leadership contest by a country mile. The other contenders were Bertie Ahern, Michael Woods and Mary O'Rourke.

Tom met repeatedly with Albert, together with Michael Smith and Charlie McCreevy, during the run-up to the election. All that matters in a leadership contest are the numbers, and those numbers must be double- and treble-checked. Pádraig Flynn, Noel Treacy and Máire Geoghegan-Quinn went about this systematically. They regularly got in contact with people they knew were not supporting Albert, not in any attempt to persuade them to change their minds, but to hammer home that their choice was respected, with the objective of ensuring that as the first two contenders were eliminated, thus sparking a second and third round, their votes would automatically transfer to Albert. If anything worried McCreevy, Smith and Tom, it was that the numbers were so overwhelmingly indicative of an Albert win.

I was hardly involved, except when the team needed something like a column ghost-written for Albert. In the brief meetings I had with him, Albert didn't parse what had been written. Low on vanity, he was task-oriented; and the task was winning the leadership, which, on 6 February 1992, he duly did. Mary O'Rourke got six votes, Woods ten and Reynolds sixty-one. The gap between Albert and the others suggested that the Fianna Fáil party was ready to unite around the businessman from Longford and that he would be Taoiseach for quite some time. It would seem that Bertie Ahern was of this view, since, despite the urging of Haughey, he refused to enter the contest.

Suddenly, our home phone was ringing as it had never rung before. Because I hate answering the phone, Tom would usually pick it up, even if he then handed the caller on to me. He didn't have to hand over many calls in the days after Albert's win. They were all for him, many of them from near-strangers, all egging to know if he was going to 'get a job' from Albert. Tom would point out that he had a job and didn't intend to give it up, and they would brush past that. No, really, was he going to get a job on Albert's team? 'I haven't a clue and I couldn't care less,' was Tom's invariable reply, delivered with increasing impatience after the first couple of days. When he went to Albert's apartment, as he did frequently, that issue never came up. What was discussed was cabinet formation. Tom made no suggestions as to who might be included, although, when Albert hopped a ball, Tom would comment on what portfolio might best suit the person named by the future Taoiseach. The second-line positions – ministers of state, then called parliamentary secretaries – were not discussed at all. Once, and only once, did Tom involve his own future in the discussion, and that was when the hopped ball had Ray Burke's name on it. Tom told Albert that he did not presume Albert would be asking him (Tom) to serve in his administration, but if he did, the appointment of Ray Burke to cabinet would ensure a refusal. Tom would not work with Burke and believed the man to be so self-evidently corrupt that his inclusion in an Albert cabinet would be so wrong that Tom couldn't be involved. Tom fair-mindedly added that this might be neither here nor there to Albert, who nodded, and they moved on.

That night, over triangular sandwiches and cups of tea in the Burlington Hotel, Michael Smith, Tom and Charlie McCreevy played around with the names likely to appear in the new cabinet. Tom told the two men what he had said to Albert about Ray Burke and they nodded. A silence fell.

'We're missing a name,' McCreevy said suddenly.

'You mean someone who'll get into cabinet? Someone we haven't mentioned at all?'

'Yep.'

'You're right,' Tom told him. Smith was looking from one to the other, trying to think of a name that had not been mentioned.

'Tell you what,' Tom said, tearing a bit of paper in half and shoving one section across the table to McCreevy. 'You write down who you think it is and I'll write down who I think it is and then we'll swap.' (The story, as later recounted to me, didn't include what Michael Smith made of his exclusion from this game.) Each wrote, folded the paper, handed it to the other, opened the one containing the other man's judgement. The name was the same on each scrap: Dr John O'Connell. Time would tell, they agreed.

None of this was shared with me, because, during that tense week, I was keeping my normal hours, starting at 4 a.m., while Tom was out at meetings until the small hours. We hardly met, although I was at home when, on 10 February 1992, Tom beckoned me, one-handed, while dialling the phone with the other.

'How would you like to get off the picket line, Diggy?' was how he opened the conversation. The reference was to the RTÉ strike, which was still going on, and the person at the other end of the line was Seán Duignan from the RTÉ newsroom. Diggy, in his startlingly handsome youth, had presented Irish dancing programmes on RTÉ before becoming an impartial and widely trusted political correspondent. Now, Tom, on behalf of the incoming Taoiseach, was testing out his attitude to sitting down at P.J. Mara's desk.

'It had not remotely occurred to me that I might be his successor,' Diggy later confessed. 'Looking back, I still wonder that I did it. It wasn't as if I was unaware of what it would involve. I had seen those fellows under pressure. More than a decade as RTÉ's "Pol Corr", operating in Leinster House with first-hand experience of the trials and tribulations of successive government press secretaries, had left me with few illusions.'

Nevertheless, helped by the advice of a friend who observed, 'You get one spin on the merry-go-round. Go for it,' Duignan agreed to meet Tom and visit Albert in his Ballsbridge apartment. As only Seán Duignan could, in the process of a high-level job interview, he managed to refer to Albert, in full Stetson, singing 'Put your Sweet Lips a Little Closer to the Phone' on Mike Murphy's TV programme. Dancing backwards as best he could from the brink, Diggy said it hadn't done Albert any harm, only to be slapped down by Albert's blunt, 'It was awful.' Shortly after the meeting, Diggy agreed to become press secretary to the new Taoiseach.

Forty-eight hours before the moment when Albert would announce his new cabinet, Dr John rang.

'Terry, you know when the cabinet will be appointed? I'm sure Tom has told you.' I didn't say that Tom didn't have to tell me, just murmured acquiescence.

'Terry, I'd really like you to be there on the day, do you know?'

'Where on the day?'

'Leinster House.'

'John, I never go near Leinster House if I can avoid it. You know that. Why would I?'

'Well, I'd really like you to be there that day.'

The penny finally dropped.

'Jesus, John, you're going to be a minister!'

'Now, Terry, I'd really like you to be there and if you go to the porter's desk someone will make sure you get to be in the right place, all right?'

'All right. Congratulations, John.'

'You promise me, now?'

'I promise.'

And so I was in a corner by the 'Bridge of Sighs' that links one part of Leinster House with another, as Albert walked by leading his cabinet towards the Dáil chamber. Máire Geoghegan-Quinn grinning and winking. P. Flynn towering over all the others, giving a magisterial nod. And, half-running, abashed and thrilled, Dr John O'Connell, who would be announced as Minister for Health.

Missing from the procession were household names like Rory O'Hanlon, Gerry Collins, Michael O'Kennedy, Mary O'Rourke, Noel Davern, Brendan Daly, Vincent Brady – and Ray Burke. Albert had changed eight people in cabinet. This radical action was probably unprecedented and has never happened since. Very significant people they were, too. Media commentators, the next day, gave Albert a taste of future coverage. Instead of viewing the move as a clean-out, as signalling a determination to refresh government, the laments were for the loss of experience and expertise from the cabinet table. The excisions were seen as punitive, and in some cases that wasn't far from the truth, but it wasn't the whole or even the essential truth.

(When, a few days later, Dermot Ahern politely asked why he was being axed as a minister of state, the answer was that he had backed the wrong horse. His removal had nothing to do with his competence, just to his having been too faithful to Haughey for too long, as Albert saw it.)

After the ceremonies, when Albert went up to the Áras to get his seal of office from the president, I went to Rory O'Hanlon's office to commiserate with him. He was tidying up his belongings in calm resignation. Having worked for him on a number of occasions, I was heartbroken that – after a period in hell as Haughey's cost-cutting Minister for Health, which had been all the more painful because

Rory was a GP himself – he should now be reduced to the ranks. As we hugged, the door to his office burst open with such force that its hinges were severely endangered, and Mary O'Rourke came into the room in a towering and vocal rage. She told me she hoped I was happy, which confused me because I was trying to remember if she'd been in the line-up of ministers and deciding that no, she had not. Since I had nothing to do with cabinet selection, I was surprised to be blamed for it, but a response of any kind was not necessary. She was in full flow and Rory and I weren't the only audience. Because she had left the door open, people passing down the checkerboard corridor slowed and in some cases stopped in order to get the full value of her fury, at the end of which she assured me that at the first opportunity she planned to tell Albert all the above.

'Fine, as long as you don't want to be a minister of state,' I said, and left.

Fair dues to her, she later acknowledged to several people – as she took up the minister of state post Albert offered her – that this might have been good advice.

I found myself on the Taoiseach's corridor, smiling at members of the Reynolds family, when Tom came up behind me, slid his arm around my waist and propelled me towards the business end of that corridor.

'You just want to see my office, don't you?'

Of course I did. Right next to the Taoiseach's office, it was. Even more impressive to me than the office I had just down the corridor from Pádraig Flynn's Minister for the Environment office in the Custom House. I had hardly registered it when he dragged me up out of the visitor's chair and led me to the next office, occupied by Bart Cronin, who had handled media relations for Reynolds when he had been Minister for Industry and Commerce. Bart immediately began preparations to offer cups of tea, while Tom asked me where I'd been. I started to tell him about the Mary O'Rourke encounter but began to falter as I watched what Bart was at. He got the kettle to boil and then hung a teacup over the spout for a few seconds before wiping it out with a tea towel and replacing it with another.

'Those cups will never physically leave this office,' Tom promised me. 'Never, as long as Bart Cronin is here. He will never wash them. He will, as you've seen, make a passing essay at sterilising them, but that's as far as it's ever going to go.'

'Look, do you fucking want a fucking cup of fucking tea or fucking not?' Cronin asked. I nodded dumbly, trying to work out how cross he was. It took a while to realise that Bart was never cross. He just fitted the f-word more often into a sentence than could any other human being I'd ever met, and I'd worked in showbiz and journalism, two of the sweariest professions around. Once you stopped noticing it, you appreciated the wit, the level of information vested in one man, the boundless courage and commitment of him and the earthy understanding of human triumph, disaster and treachery to be found in rural anecdotes. Bart also had a grasp of the ballot box realities of every county that was up there with McCreevy's. He asked me some question about my husband's Machiavellian mind, which left me clutching a freshly sanitised cuppa which actually tasted fine, mesmerised by him and Tom dunking Marietta biscuits into theirs and then fishing for the slop. References to Machiavelli didn't compute.

'He means Diggy,' Tom said.

'What about Diggy?'

Bart explained that Tom Savage was putting Diggy in front of the media not because Diggy would be good at fucking manipulating fucking media or delivering any fucking subtle fucking interpretations, but because Diggy had one fucking trait that was bleeding obvious even to a fucking journalist. The 'bleeding' wobbled me slightly but I asked him what the trait was. Innocence, he told me. Imfuckingpregnable innocence. Bart went through a list of former press secretaries he did not believe had shared that innocence and Tom sat, head down, smiling and saying nothing.

As we walked downstairs, accosted on every step by TDs, senators and their families, we were silent, but when we got into the car, I asked him if Bart's rationale was why Tom had picked Seán Duignan.

'Yes, but not for the reason Bart attaches to it,' Tom said, saluting the security guys by name as they lowered the spiked obstacle to let his car out of the Leinster House grounds. 'Although that's part of it. Nothing wrong with appointing a man uncomfortable with lying who would be obvious about it if he was put to it. But the key reason is that Diggy doesn't want power. He doesn't want to show off. He's already famous and he'll be dead happy for me and Bart to be working in the background on things he doesn't need to know about and wouldn't want to know about. He's also bright enough to know what he doesn't know while smart enough to ask for help when he needs it.'

Within days, the administration was mired in controversy around the X case, and that was just the beginning of a chaotic – although in some key respects profoundly contributory – period in office for Albert Reynolds. This was almost exclusively Tom's gig, and although he continued to lead training courses in the company, he was less present and that meant that I had to take on some of his tasks. Additionally, it meant that I had no more knowledge of what was going on in Government Buildings than any member of the general public. Tom went to the North many times during this period to meet old colleagues from his days working for a peace organisation, but he said nothing about this aspect of the job, other than to praise Albert's commitment to peace on the island and to refer to the Taoiseach having 'the courage of his ignorance', an admiring phrase I later incorporated into one of Albert's speeches. Tom spent a lot of time over late-night cups of tea trying to explain loyalties on the ground in the North, without, he felt, greatly enhancing the Taoiseach's understanding of the complexities involved.

'I remind myself of a thing you said about Gay's researchers,' he said one evening. 'D'you remember, you told me some of them were a bit ashamed that Gay didn't have a degree, and wanted him to be better educated? They were wrong. Gay needs only curiosity and courage. And Albert likewise.'

Later Tom tried to explain to the civil servants in the Taoiseach's office that when Albert demanded briefings to last no longer than one page, it was not because the man was shallow or uncommitted. Tom circulated the memo Winston Churchill had sent to *his* civil servants, demanding brevity and succinctness from them, but amusedly noted the element of Cover Your Ass in longer briefings; dealing with an impulsive and impatient political leader in Ireland created an incentive to obviate the possibility of subsequent reproach, were the leader to take flawed action based on incomplete data. One of Churchill's many biographers, Erik Larson, has observed that demanding precise communication 'installed at all levels a new sense of responsibility for events', an outcome Albert may not have articulated, but would certainly have wanted.

Tom liked the fact that Albert was a bundle of goodwill, impatience and obstinacy, 'not shackled by the rigidity of political ideology'.

For the most part, the civil servants liked Tom and he liked them, not least because he had seen how effectively the civil service north of the border operated when power was taken back to Westminster, leaving them effectively in total charge. So he was startled, one morning about three months into his time as Albert's communications adviser, when an assistant secretary came into his office in Government Buildings like a fully formed tornado and demanded his expense sheets.

'Let's not worry about expense sheets,' Tom said.

'I *have* to worry about expense sheets.'

'Well, you won't be getting any from me.'

She drew a deep breath, fixed him with a glare, and told him the Mara era was over. Tom did the characteristic one-handed wipe of his open face, gestured for her to sit down and waited until she did so before asking what she meant by referring to 'the Mara era'. Through gritted teeth, she spoke of a time when an adviser to the Taoiseach had billed the Taoiseach's office for the dry-cleaning of his clothes, the purchase of wine, more taxis than it seemed possible for one man to use and a rake of other expenses which, as far as she was concerned, had nothing to do with his departmental functioning. Tom laughed and didn't tell her it was he who had suggested to Albert that to ensure a civilised handover from the Haughey administration, Mara should be retained for the first six months after Albert's inauguration. (I had fought him on this, but had been ignored. When Albert and Tom were minded to be magnanimous, small-minded naysayers like me had no influence.) As the senior civil servant opened her mouth to say more, Tom leaned forward in his classic stance – forearms on thighs, hands hanging loosely between his knees.

'I won't be giving you expense sheets. If I have expenses, I'll cover them myself. This role may not be important, but it's a privilege and, in that context, it would be – it would be egregious to seek expenses. And that's an end to it.'

With luck, the civil servant – a formidable executive who went on to higher things in that and other departments – saw this as nobility on Tom's part. Which may have been part of it, in fairness. But the main reason was that he couldn't be bothered keeping receipts and filling out forms. Life was too short. But then, the way Tom saw it, life was too short to be fighting to be in the background (or the foreground) of every photograph or to be present at every meeting the Taoiseach had with international leaders. He sat in a little at the beginning, enough to predict that history would be kind to Albert.

'He likes people,' he said. 'He doesn't force people to prove themselves to him. He assumes they're going to like him and it gives him a great ease with other leaders. He never sets out to be impressive.'

One of the leaders Albert didn't set out to impress but with whom he nonetheless developed a good relationship was John Major, Britain's prime minister. Tom later said that the two men had 'changed the way Britain and Ireland looked at each other and treated each other'. On the face of it, the elegant and apparently bland Major and Albert the dancehall promoter had nothing in common. In fact, they had enormous swatches of commonality in their biographies. Albert might know every ragged dancehall in Ireland, but Major knew every town hall in the United Kingdom, because his parents were music hall artists. He never concealed it – in fact he later wrote a fine book about music hall as an entertainment genre – but it was somehow elided in the public view of him, which was a pity. The two leaders found in each other an unpretentious confidence that made for mutual trust.

That level of trust never developed between Albert and the Irish media. The first six months' coverage of the new Taoiseach was a freshet of condemnation. This, despite the fact that the media had, ostensibly at least, wanted rid of Charlie Haughey and had no favoured alternative candidate to replace him. No matter how negative had been the public portrayal of Haughey, there could be no doubt about an odd residual nostalgia for aspects of his persona. In the early days of working out who would succeed CJ, Charlie McCreevy had worried about the electability of Albert because the Roscommon man had no smell of cordite off him. He was absolutely faithful to Kathleen, his wife, and constantly concerned for her during the months when she was being treated for breast cancer. He adored his two sons and five daughters. Tom said that anybody who knew Albert Reynolds 'knew his family was always his first love and preoccupation'.

It was as if this, together with his very accessibility, had been acceptable when he was a minister or in opposition, but now he was in power, now he had cut away such a huge number of ministers with whom the media was familiar, it – together with his dancehall background – evoked a provincialism media didn't cotton on to. When Mrs Reynolds told a journalist that she couldn't figure how Albert could, within three weeks, 'have gone from being the best man around to someone none of us recognise', one of the most prominent columnists described what she said in the most unprovably pejorative terms: as an 'outburst' that was part of a media campaign.

For whatever reason, Albert got not even the briefest media honeymoon. It didn't help that he decided the media were all agin him and that preparing for interviews was, accordingly, a waste of time. This, in turn, led to less than productive media outings. On one occasion, when

I happened to hear Albert interviewed by Shane Kenny on RTÉ's *News at One*, I rang Seán Duignan because I couldn't reach Tom.

'Jesus, Seán, that was a disaster,' I told him. 'Albert was abrasive, argumentative and pushy.'

Seán politely told me he didn't think it was that bad. I didn't argue with him, for two reasons. You can't argue with someone as sweet-natured as Seán Duignan. And it also struck me at the time that he was dealing with an unprecedented media frenzy and that he didn't need me, from a position of safe outsider ignorance, telling him how to do his job. I shut up. I did, a little later, tell Tom that he should stop Albert saying whatever was in his head to the media. The minute I said it, I regretted it. Tom silently beckoned me into our sitting room and gestured for me to sit down.

'Tess, don't say anything like that to me again,' he told me. 'When you work with Pádraig Flynn on a communications issue, the two of you get to a particular point, and when you pick up the next time you meet him, he's still at that point, right?'

I nodded at what seemed obvious and universal.

'Albert is different. That doesn't happen with him. If I get Albert to a particular point and he delivers on it, that's the end of it. When we start up again, he has reverted to his first position. There is nothing I can do about that. I am doing my best to get the best out of a good man. Now leave it alone, okay?'

It was partly that instruction, but mainly how busy I was with other clients, that ensured I never knew the details of Tom's involvement in the peace process and other issues. Although I was aware that Tom had been the priest sent by Cardinal Conway in 1969 to welcome the British army to Northern Ireland, I never knew the details of his later involvement in the peace process and other issues. One of the other issues was decriminalising homosexuality, which Reynolds had said was 'at the bottom of my list of priorities' even though Ireland was in violation of the European Convention on Human Rights for several years when he became Taoiseach.

'Tom Savage, an instinctive liberal who had regularly urged the Taoiseach to decriminalise homosexuality, now saw his opportunity,' wrote Seán Duignan later. 'Reynolds grumbled and warned that such as former Minister Noel Davern had clearly indicated he would not support decriminalisation. Apart from Reynolds putting down that perfunctory marker, Savage found that he was now practically pushing an open door on the issue.'

Tom said later that this open door was one of the reasons he admired Albert so much: 'a deeply committed Catholic himself, he was prepared to take risks in the interest of human rights and the country.'

12

Body Language, Lies and Crisis

You know the story if you're a buyer of airport business success books. The brilliant entrepreneur spots a gap in the market. Does research to confirm the gap exists. Designs a product or service to meet the need. Provides the product or service and – like the proverbial mousetrap – purchasers beat a path to their door, and rightly so.

As a believer in this model, in the early 1990s, the gap was obvious to me. Lying. Or, more precisely, the detection of lying. Some sectors of society had a serious need to be able to spot a liar at ten paces: gardaí, people working in human resources, job or promotion interview panels. The publication of a handful of bullshit books about body language irrevocably but wrongly convinced their readers that they could interpret the movements of another person with deadly accuracy.

People who believe in body language are like people who believe in homeopathy. It doesn't matter how far against them the scientific evidence goes, they're converts, tattooed with beliefs they cannot relinquish without damage to their self-esteem. Faith in body language interpretation repeatedly surfaces in the commentary on Big Debates, where journalists who believe themselves to simply deal in facts slide sideways into unproven interpretation in their desire to find one contender a loser: never mind what they said, look at the way they put their forefingers to their lips or ran their hand through their hair.

'Body language' is the elevation of basic observation and subjective judgement into pseudoscience. The covers of any of the popular books on the topic sum up just how far they are from science. While promising purchasers that they will never be lied to again (implication: the book will teach the reader to spot 'tells' which will reveal every time anybody utters an untruth to them) they are riddled with whatever-you're-having-yourself question marks. One of the funnier visuals on the cover of a hardback currently on sale shows individuals in a number of poses. The guy in the middle has his hands clasped in front of his scrotum. 'Protecting his manhood?' asks the caption beside the illustration. To which the answer has to be 'Well, yes, if you must ask the bleeding obvious.'

Most of the deadly 'tells' explicated in the books on the subject are simple, obvious and usually wrong. One of them is the shot of the guy with folded arms. This appears in one of those videos that pop up on the web promising to improve your pitches and presentations. The minute you see your boss sitting like this, goes the advice, over a sequence of a man seated, arms folded, with a face like thunder, you need to stop and ask him why he is so hostile, as revealed by his body language. According to the pseudoscience of body language, the minute you see folded arms, you are doomed. Folded arms are a dead giveaway. If members of an audience fold their arms, you're done as a speech-maker. Never mind that at any given time, some members of every audience fold their arms. Never mind that it may be caused by a myriad of factors unrelated to you, like the air conditioning being too cold. Never mind that looking out for arm placement might distract you from much more relevant information, like the mutual glance between audience members that says 'Did you ever hear such a load of …?'

Any good actor will look askance if asked in rehearsal to first assemble their character's body language, because body language is an inevitable outcome of character, not the precursor. The late Donal McCann, playing a British officer in a Boucicault melodrama, conveyed his formal shyness on the first night by rising slightly on his toes when his character was under pressure. It was odd, idiosyncratic, funny. Nobody had ever seen a shy person do it. It simply emerged from his understanding of the man he was playing. It showed up on the first night to the fury of the other actors in the show, not because McCann was a scene stealer, although the other performers clearly believed this was the reason, but because it was only then that the totality of the character came together for him.

Communications consultants tend to find body language surfacing in two facets of their business – or I do, anyway. The first is when clients want to be taught it. For example, someone who has little real confidence in themselves will want to know how to enter a room or behave physically at a meeting in a way that bespeaks authority. This is where the consultant can refer the client to a therapist to address their self-esteem issues or simply train them in the behaviours that will help make others take them seriously. 'Stand up straight, meet their eye, shake their hand firmly, don't fidget and stop licking your lips,' would summarise most of these behaviours, but, oddly, getting people to internalise and deliver on the summary takes time and practice. Entering a room looking confident is simpler.

The second instance where body language turns up is when the media wants to prove that someone, usually but not always a politician, is lying, and believe that any number of readily identifiable 'tells' will reveal all. Up goes footage of the subject inserting a finger inside their shirt collar. Gotcha. Clearly discomfited by their own lying. Or footage of the subject's leg bouncing as if they were listening to a Sousa march. Or footage of the subject putting her hand over her mouth.

A 'body language expert' will always be available to claim that any one of these indicates that the subject is lying. Which is complete nonsense. Men insert their fingers inside their shirt collars as if to loosen them for many reasons, including recent weight gain. Each one of us knows someone with a rhythmic leg we'd love to amputate. Its constant jiggling has no relevance to the veracity of what its owner is saying. Putting a hand over your mouth is a similar irrelevancy. Even if someone demonstrates all three simultaneously, what is illustrated is that the person is nervous and under pressure – as is likely when a politician goes on mainstream mass media.

That's not to say that a physical behaviour cannot be outed as false. The nineteenth-century neurologist Guillaume Duchenne worked out that when someone is only pretending to smile, they don't get bunching under the lower eyelids as the cheek rises and creates pressure. It is possible, therefore, to state with certainty, faced with a series of photographs, which are genuine and which are false smiles. Useful? Not terribly.

The other revealing body language was identified by the Federal Bureau of Investigation (FBI). Looking at closed circuit footage of accused individuals in prison cells, and matching the footage to the history of each case, they found an odd and interesting pattern. Innocent people, left in a cell for a couple of hours, paced and fidgeted and even cried. Guilty people went to sleep.

The American who did the most interesting work on body language coming into the twenty-first century was Stan Walters, who apprehended that many of the signals being interpreted as indicative – or, indeed, probative – of lying were in fact signals of general stress. 'All deception signals, either verbal or nonverbal, are a form of stress, but not all stress signs indicate lying,' he wrote.

We liked the evidence-based approach of Walters and came to an informal agreement with him that if we created and sold a course incorporating some of his research, he would become a delivery partner. Then we developed a course, recorded illustrative videos, trained trainers and contacted the target market with our brilliant new offering, confident that after the excitedly positive reactions of the pilot participants, we were home and hosed.

We weren't. Nobody wanted the course. In a decade, we managed to sell it only twice. We never found out if the obstacle was people's pre-existing but unjustified confidence in their own ability to spot liars; we just found out that, while most of our courses sold themselves and then sold themselves again in the form of referred business, the course about detecting lying sat like a dead thing in our brochure and later – briefly – online. So much for the theory about identifying a gap in the market.

Fortunately, at around the same time, another business stream presented itself to us, unsought. This was crisis communications, and came first in the form of a panicked phone call from a company that had, the night before, suffered an explosion that had blown up a substantial part of the plant. We controlled ourselves as we listened and didn't use the great Michael Caine line about only being supposed to blow the bloody doors off. We were glad we hadn't, because as we interrogated the incident, it became complicated and frightening, involving chemicals leaking into the local sewage system and key interested parties being ignorant of the whole incident.

I went through what had happened with the managing director after telling the PR person that she simply didn't have enough data to safely handle this one. More and more damaging details emerged. I listed the authorities the MD needed to inform right away and told him I'd be there three hours later. I was. The plant was surrounded by fire engines and police cars and the managing director was immured with members of both forces. Someone got a message to him that I had arrived and he sought a 'comfort break' to cover meeting me, wasting several minutes of that corridor meeting giving out to me for drawing the cops on him, even though he knew involving them was inevitable. Handing him the list of instructions he needed to give to his management to co-operate with me, I told him I'd be happy to take the train back to Dublin and not charge him any further fee. (That was code for 'You already owe me several thousand and being pettish about the issue won't save you any money.') He issued the instructions and went back into his office for more torture from the boys and girls in blue.

The first instruction he had given his managers, drawn from my list, was to provide a war room. This had to be a big enough room to contain as many as twenty people, equipped with easels and the capacity to stick large sheets of paper on the wall. Plus a constantly renewed source of coffee and a note-taker. To be nothing but honest, I stole this idea from true crime books I had read, but it worked a treat.

The note-taker was thrilled by the job and invaluable. It was she who told me who was in charge of different functions within the plant, who would have been on duty the previous night, and whether or not the managing director had already talked to them. Called in, one by one, they explained what had happened and what action they had taken. They were, although they didn't know it, responding to Rudyard Kipling's 'six honest serving men': the questions What, Why, Where, When, Who and How. Those questions are pivotal to journalism, but they're also vital to getting a corporate story straight in a crisis. Within an hour, the sheets around the walls told that story, and each of the managers involved came back to confirm and in some cases to correct that story. Half of them fought with me over what I was doing. It would suit me better, was the message, to put out a statement indicating that their standards were superb, that nobody had been killed or seriously injured and that this was the first explosion they had ever experienced. I told them I appreciated their advice. It is always civil to thank people for advice you don't intend to follow. Fighting with them rarely makes them feel better about you ignoring their wisdom.

By late afternoon, a statement was ready and the decision had been made to leave the on-camera talking to the fire service and the guards, who were thrilled to death with the opportunity to talk about how fast and effective their response had been. The note-taker took dictation from me as to recommended company actions for the following few weeks, including how they were going to communicate with their staff, who hadn't figured much in corporate thinking. Then I got on the train and went home. The invoice sent was promptly paid and neither the company nor the general public heard of them again, which was a great outcome for all concerned.

Even better, though, was the fact that by accident, and while being paid, we had invented a new product – crisis management – which not only sold well but became a distinguishing feature of our then company and our later company, The Communications Clinic. Explosions happen. Emissions happen. Fires happen. All of them, in fairness and in tribute to better laws and emergency services, happen much less frequently than they used to. Boats break up (as Linda Cullen of COCO Television found during the making of a TV series). Bosses sexually assault employees. Frauds are committed. Bankruptcy is experienced. Blackmail is perpetrated. Each of these requires a crisis communications response that follows a pattern we developed twenty-five years ago, with added speed because of social media. Each also requires resolution in the face of predictable corporate response.

Concealment is the overwhelmingly likely reaction on the part of managers who instinctively believe that the rules set down by regulators must be met but minimally. Don't give anybody any more information than the law or the regulations demand, and – while you demand that internal and external communications professionals immediately get the company out of this spot of bother – don't tell them anything much, either. This approach inevitably leads to a 'drip, drip' release of data that pisses off everybody, including staff, who don't want continuing questions about the place where they work, and the communications professionals, who look ropy in front of the media.

Corporate crises irresistibly reveal the truth about the commitment to communication of the corporation involved. The ones who regard their communications department as a subservient arm of the marketing function don't ask the people from that department to take over in a crisis, preferring to handle it themselves (*here be dragons*), and instruct the PR people to do the impossible, like prevent the story appearing at all. They might then pull in external consultants who will, if they're any good, tell them to get a grip and lay out the communication that must be done and who must do it.

The other factor revealed in a crisis is how well the organisation relates to its own employees. If it relates poorly to them, it is creating its own whistleblowers. Those whistleblowers will be speedily located by legacy and indeed social media and the details they will add to the saga will not be helpful to the company or organisation.

Blackmail, of course, is one of the most interesting crises to face an employer and an employee. How we dealt with one political blackmail case will be dealt with in the next chapter.

13

BLACKMAIL

The first time Dr John O'Connell figured out that Albert Reynolds knew Tom or any of us was when he sat on his right at a Fianna Fáil parliamentary party meeting.

'He had a Carr Communications folder,' Dr John told me long afterwards. 'That was the first time I saw your name. Once I saw it, I knew he had been up to see you.'

John, although he was a volatile and talkative man, was also good with secrets, so he shut up about this observation. At this early stage in his membership of Fianna Fáil, he was learning and informing Charlie Haughey of what he assumed the leader should know. Part of that observation was of Albert when the latter was asked some technical question about the workings of his department.

'[The answer] came out like machine gun fire,' John remembered. 'All facts and figures, and they were all delighted with it. I said to Haughey, I said "Albert's very good, he's able to rattle off." He said, "Yeah, but he won't write a speech. I'm trying to get him to write speeches. You say he's so good, you get him to write speeches. But he won't do it."'

John, who knew that Haughey never wrote a speech in his life, despite the vanity publication of a doorstopper compilation of Dr

Mansergh's work for him, had the smarts to leave Albert alone on this one. Later on, he found out that the best method for Albert speech-making started with someone (me, in many cases) sitting in front of him with two recording devices (because I am nothing if not anxious) asking him questions about the topic on which he was to speak, capturing all the facts and figures and pulling it together, using his own words, into a coherent speech he could read and deliver.

The day on which Albert became Taoiseach and fired eight former ministers was preceded by a summons to John O'Connell. He was to come to the new Taoiseach's office.

'We're making you Minister for Health,' Albert told him. 'Don't put your foot in it.'

It was the pinnacle of achievement, as John saw it. All his Christmases coming together on one day, all his hopes and dreams arriving with a seal and a trip to Áras an Uachtaráin with his new cabinet colleagues. Dr John, the man whose mother could not read or write, whose siblings had died of TB, who had been mocked by fellow students in medical school for his squeaky plastic shoes, had made it into power. He left Albert's room unsurprised but awed, not knowing where he was supposed to go next. Someone pointed him to a room with a half-open door. In he went.

'All these ex-ministers are there. And one of them – Ray Burke – asked me "What are *you* doing up here?" As if I had no right, like I was always being told: I had no right. Because only ministers were supposed to be on that floor. And I said Albert had called me and made me Minister for Health. It dawned on them then.'

What dawned on Burke and the others was that Albert was appointing people first, before he told the existing ministers their fate. They had been summoned to attend, but each TD who followed John O'Connell down from the Taoiseach's office, newly appointed to a department, meant one less appointment for the waiting group until finally it was clear: they were done. Nobody seems to know what Albert's motivation was for this untypical sequence. John was too excited and impressed by his own appointment and the protocols around it to ask. The media and Fianna Fáil were agog trying to figure out how Dr John had done it, but, although Tom Savage, Máire Geoghegan-Quinn, Charlie McCreevy, Pádraig Flynn and Noel Treacy were aware of Albert's reluctance, not to say resistance, when told of Seán Doherty's impending broadcast confession, none of them felt the need to share that oddity – with, as Justin O'Brien, in his book about Haughey, *The Modern Prince*, says, 'the inevitable inference that he had some undertaking in advance of that confession that Haughey would go on an agreed date, and feared that the undertaking would be unravelled by Doherty's unexpected move.'

Even though I was a close friend of Dr John over a long period, I didn't know the truth at the time, one of the reasons being that John immediately immersed himself in his department and we hardly spoke. It was long after he had left office and was living the most obscure life money could buy that he told me what had led to him owning a written commitment from Charles Haughey to resign as Taoiseach on a stated day.

The reality was that Dr John had two threats to hang over Charles Haughey's head. The first and more disgraceful action from a prime minister when in office, was taking €50,000 in 1965 (worth more than €100,000 today) donated by a Saudi nobleman and billionaire – and friend of O'Connell. John had facilitated the donation and bought into the pretence under which it was given. John should not have been the third man in this transaction, and Haughey should never have taken the money.

Much later, when Brian Lenihan Sr became desperately ill, John hit up wealthy friends and added their money to his own to create a sizeable sum that enabled Lenihan to access the best American treatment. John was so delighted with his fundraising that he sought a meeting with Haughey in the Taoiseach's office, bringing the banknotes in a bulging briefcase to show CJ, who was encomiastic but was interrupted halfway through their meeting by an incoming call from Margaret Thatcher. John was ushered into an anteroom. Haughey dealt with Thatcher, then called out to John to rejoin him. When John got to the bank, later on, to lodge the donated money, he found it was short by €20,000. That left him heart-struck. He might have gone along with the notion of Haughey being latter-day royalty, entitled to whatever he demanded of his subjects (although Sheikh Fustok certainly wasn't among those subjects), but to steal money from a dying friend was beyond despicable.

From that day forth, John O'Connell became Haughey's most dangerous enemy. When the time was right, as he saw it, he reminded Haughey of the sheikh's gift and told him he knew about Haughey stealing money from Lenihan, a man who – before he became ill – was a biddable mouth for Haughey, always willing to go out on the media to defend his leader, even if it required him articulating a variant on the truth and sometimes talking nonsense that got him widely caricatured. That didn't matter to Haughey. As far as Dr John was concerned, nothing but money mattered to Haughey, who consequently could not be allowed to continue as Taoiseach. Neither I nor Tom had any clue that this was going on, or that John, having revealed what he knew and would publicly reveal if Haughey didn't agree in writing to go, delivered a deadline to the Taoiseach, around which the latter wriggled for some days. But John was angry and determined and would not negotiate. Haughey eventually signed a handwritten letter for John on Department of the Taoiseach notepaper. This letter – handed to Albert by Dr John – promised Haughey's resignation on a date a few months later than turned out to be the case. Possession of that letter was what caused Albert to shout at Tom on the night of the Doherty confession, demanding he stop the event, because Albert thought it would put a spanner in the works neatly orchestrated by Dr John.

One of the characteristics of John O'Connell was that the past was ever-present to him, and so, when he was filling me in on all of this plotting and planning, he became tearfully furious all over again about him sitting in front of the briefcase – a small suitcase, really – in the bank and the bank officials looking puzzled about the money being so much less than he had told them it would be. He was not furious about the embarrassment. He was furious that a man would not only steal from his most loyal friend but do it at a time when the friend had an existential need of the money.

He didn't do it to get the Health portfolio, although he made no secret of his delight when payback came in that form. The delight died almost immediately, as it became apparent to Dr John that despite all his idealism, all his experience, all his in-depth knowledge of every medical system around, he could not hack it in the Department of Health and was to become, in his own sad description, 'the worst ever Minister for Health'.

Just how badly the dream turned to nightmare was partly concealed by the turbulence on almost all fronts that characterised Albert's two short years as Taoiseach. Controversy dogged Albert, particularly the Beef Tribunal, which raised questions about his ethics and which came to a generally unsatisfactory conclusion. The only time I was in John's Department of Health office I was appalled by the relationship he had with those of his senior civil servants who were trying to explain why a course of action he wanted was not possible. The civil servants were not doing a *Yes, Minister* attempt to confuse him, but the elaborate detail and bloodless language they quite properly used drove John nuts and he made *ad hominem* attacks on them, which were shocking to watch. When I tried to intervene, simply to achieve clarity, he got emotional and accused me of being on their side. I told him he knew that wasn't the case and left.

I was later to experience a more constant, indeed commercial, relationship with another health minister who went into the awful (and unhealthy) offices then housing the department. Dr James Reilly went in there with great plans, including one to essentially remodel the health service, or at least the acute hospital sector, along the successful lines of the Dutch equivalent. He was spat out by the system, defeated for different reasons. Brian Cowen, himself a less than successful health minister, was right when he described the place as 'Angola', observing that a minister could leave a clean desk on a Friday only for catastrophe to hit from an unexpected angle over the weekend.

John was unsuccessful as minister, although that was not painfully obvious to the public or media during his tenure. After the disastrous encounter in his office, I kept clear of him, not wishing him anything but good, but knowing I couldn't help him achieve that good. What I didn't know was the impact on his ministerial career of his disability. In fact, at the time I didn't know about the disability. He was profoundly deaf in one ear and in deep denial about this. He constantly misunderstood what people were saying to him, having not shared with them the fact that he would find them hard to hear. Once he misunderstood a point, he regarded any attempt to reorient his comprehension as insulting to his competence. This led to harrowing breakdowns in working relationships, with willing servitors turning into deadly enemies because they believed he had mistreated them. He had all the underdog suspicions of a poor man, even though he was a rich man. Worst of all, the relationship with Albert Reynolds went down the tubes because of this problem. At the cabinet table, other members of the government couldn't believe that a relationship that had started out with such mutual trust could turn so snappy and impatient on both sides. The two men sat side by side at the table. Some of those present knew that Albert was almost completely deaf in one ear. Some of those present worked out from experience that Dr John was equally if not more deaf in one ear. What nobody knew was that the seating meant John's deaf ear was on the same side as Albert's deaf ear, so neither could properly hear the other.

None of which was apparent to me, so my attitude was one of shrugging inattention, until the day when John rang me and said he had to meet me urgently and could it be in my home, for confidentiality? Of course, I said, and we sorted the time. (Clients came to our house frequently enough for Anton, our son, as a seven- or eight-year-old, to adopt a drill of opening the door to them, sitting them down and offering them coffee or tea.)

When John arrived, I offered the coffee or tea and he opted for the tea. Handing it to him, I realised his hands were shaking and immediately wondered whether this was Parkinson's or anxiety. It turned out to be anxiety. He had to get out of the cabinet immediately, he told me. He was being blackmailed. I drank my coffee and waited. Somebody who had been close to him had decided to make public details of a financial settlement to which the other person had agreed. John produced the documentation, which was extensive and took me some time to grasp. Even when I did grasp it, it didn't make sense, because the settlement, marking nothing more than an agreement to go their separate business ways, was exceptionally generous, setting the other person up for life.

'I don't understand why they feel cheated,' I said.

John shook his head and tried to re-order the papers in front of him with his still-shaking hands. No, no, he said, the individual didn't feel cheated. They had signed documents indicating that the financial settlement was acceptable. (He found those documents in the pile and showed them to me.) It was that, *post factum*, they were unhappy with the relationship ending and planned to humiliate him for that.

'But how would it humiliate you to be exposed as having been generous?'

Near tears, he told me that he could not be blackmailed by the threat of any financial revelations or any other revelations. The threat – the blackmail opportunity – lay in the other person knowing that John would rather die than have personal details spewed all over the media, even if those personal details would not bring him into public disrepute.

'Why would any of this require you to resign from cabinet?'

He looked at me as if I was stupid, which I was, pointing out that it was only as a minister, only as a prominent public figure, that he was vulnerable. If he went back to being an ordinary Joe Soap, where was the story? I suggested that someone who was obviously in the white heat of revenge-seeking might, even if John stopped being a minister, still try to place their story in the media, but he was dismissive of this possibility. No journalist reading the documentation would find him guilty of anything, and why would anybody publish unharmful material about a private citizen? We to'd and fro'd about this for some time, but it was impossible to shift him. Only cabinet resignation would do. Why, I asked, did he need my help with resigning from government? He was more than capable of writing the pro forma letter to achieve that.

He explained that it had to be done in secret, and gave me another look implying that I was an egregiously slow learner. It had to be done in secret, because a sudden resignation would provoke journalists to investigate the motivation behind it, thereby providing a market for the individual who wanted to do him down. Postponing it in any way was not going to work, first of all because he didn't want to lie about the cause, although he saw no reason to talk about the cause. Even though his health wasn't great, he was not prepared to claim he was resigning due to bad health. The big problem was Albert.

That surprised me because I couldn't see where Albert fitted into this dilemma except as a recipient of a letter of resignation. John explained that Albert could persuade him, John, to do anything. He was putty in his hands. Albert would not want him to resign and would turn him inside out with argument until John agreed to withdraw his letter of resignation.

Now that he had hospital-passed the entirety of this issue to me, the shake in his hands slowed down and he hit a condition of resigned calm. I would sort it, he was confident of that. I wasn't. Headlights lit up the big-windowed room and John leaped to his feet as if the KGB was coming to abduct him. Where could he go, he wanted to know. What room could he hide in?

The headlights went off and Tom got out of his car. John shrank back into his chair, mortified by his own terror. Tom hugged him and – typical of Tom – asked no questions, filling the awkward silence while I cleared the table and made more tea with a funny story about Albert bullying ministers about their pre-Budget figures.

'May not be an economist, but Albert sure knows his figures,' Tom said before leaving the room with the excuse that he had an urgent appointment with the television to watch a match. He disappeared, leaving John sipping tea and nibbling a biscuit and me making coffee.

And that's when it hit me. I came back to the table with every detail of the solution in my head.

'What's the one day the Taoiseach cannot pay the smallest attention to John O'Connell?' I asked. John shook his head, baffled. Budget Day, I told him, and he nodded, agreeing but not satisfied. Budget Day was about ten days away.

'Park that for the moment. You have a place in London?'

I knew he did, because John was obsessed with his health, perhaps to the point of hypochondria, and was comfortable only when he was a five-minute London cab drive from the London Clinic. He could head for that city, turn off all phones except the landline in his London apartment, the number of which Albert didn't know, and his letter of resignation could be delivered to the Taoiseach's office first thing in the morning on Budget Day, announcing to the Taoiseach that, as of the moment of its reception, John O'Connell was neither a minister nor a TD. Albert would be furious, of course, and would tell his staff to get O'Connell on the phone immediately. None of John's numbers would answer. Albert might go so far as to request that someone go to John's address, although neither of us thought that likely. He would, however, because he was clever, talk to Department of Health officials to see if they knew anything or had an extra number for John. John didn't think Albert had the numbers of any of his children but doubted Albert would ever seek to contact him through them, and Albert knew John had no significant other.

John and I worked through every move on paper and interrogated the rules that must be obeyed if this was to be done properly. We discussed Albert's reactions. He would be livid and – John admitted – somewhat distracted during Budget Day, which John regretted in advance, but a Taoiseach doesn't have that much that is crucial to do on Budget Day, or the day after. That usually falls to the Minister for Finance (and, these days, the Minister for Public Expenditure and Reform) with the line ministers filling the radio programmes on the second day. Albert would not fail to do his job in that forty-eight-hour period, at the end of which, John predicted, the Taoiseach would have moved on and possibly even be glad to have an influential position to offer someone else who might be better at it. If the forty-eight hours around Budget Day could be managed tightly, John's political career would be over and done with in an odd but muted way. If.

I knocked on the door of the room where our TV was, Tom came out to give John a parting hug, and off went the Merc that had come from the Brunei fleet. John and I were constantly on the phone to each other during the following ten days, identifying factors requiring a workaround. What was most obvious, every time we talked, was how he had already reverted to the best of himself. He wasn't fighting with his officials about anything. He fought the good last-minute fight about what money the department would get. He didn't do anything inappropriately final. Then, the day before Budget Day, he flew to London and went incommunicado. The mechanics of the plan went into effect and it worked seamlessly. By the time anybody other than Albert knew about John's departure, it was a minor puzzle hardly worth exploring. I doubt if Albert even discussed it with Tom. Tom certainly didn't discuss it with me. My husband was possessed only of functional curiosity. (Unlike his son, who does a generalised hoovering up of anything interesting and can retrieve and re-use it years hence.)

Tom did silently put a newspaper, folded to a small story about John's resignation, in front of me at home, but that was it.

14

A Great, Rainy Day

Early on in Albert's tenure, a group of gay activists came to see me. I had prepared some of them for high-profile media outings like the famous *Late Late Show* where Gay made his splendid off-the-cuff response to a bigot in the audience who wanted to know why 'homosexuals' were 'obsessed with other men's back passages'. Gay crisply told him that a lot of straight men were obsessed with women's front passages, which managed to be crushing in its matching crudity.

The gay men sitting around our boardroom a while later were deeply depressed. What was wrong, I asked. Máire Geoghegan-Quinn, was the response. The new Minister for Justice. *Fianna Fáil* Minister for Justice. She would, they predicted, set the whole movement towards equality back a decade, if not more. They talked of her with the absolute conviction that she would continue the Fianna Fáil pattern of squarely ignoring EU regulations on this subject.

I began to laugh, which briefly offended them. No, no, no, I told them. I knew her well. Well enough to know that she was the solution to their problem, not the other way round. But how could they reach her? I was looking around at a bunch of bright, argumentative, well-informed men of various ages. None of them was right for the job. Then it struck me to suggest that two mothers of gay sons might together seek an audience with the minister, to talk to her about the subject. Phil Moore and Patricia Kilroy were asked and were willing. Phil had been a prominent feminist and political activist and Patricia was a wonderful painter in watercolours. Each had a gay son. Both were the kind of calm, quietly convincing personalities Máire Geoghegan-Quinn would listen to. They sent a request to her office. She met them. They talked. She questioned. They talked some more. At the end, she promised them that she would speedily decriminalise homosexuality. And she did. The fact that it was long overdue and that, as a nation state within the European Union, we had to do it sooner or later, should not detract from the fact that this was a TD in a morally conservative party, and one from the West of Ireland at that. That was Máire Geoghegan-Quinn for you.

For the most part, I tended to deal with Albert's ministers, like Máire and Pádraig Flynn, rather than with the Taoiseach himself. Working with Flynn rarely posed a problem, except when his minister of state, Mary Harney, who occupied an office in the Custom House a floor down and a corridor away from the minister's, asked that I visit her in her office. Now, at any age and any stage in her career, Mary Harney was and is an interesting bundle of molecules. She doesn't do charm. She can be generous, helpful, funny, and I have enjoyed all of those from her, but she none of the glad-handing, elbow-clutching, first-names-and-favours approach typical of her party of origin, Fianna Fáil, back when she started. She just is Mary Harney and you can like it or lump it.

I was fascinated by her oratorical strength. The first leader of the Progressive Democrats, Des O'Malley, came to our company to be prepared for his initial ard fheis. Bunny drilled him so well in how to use autocue that the following day Conor Cruise O'Brien, in the newspaper for which he wrote, praised O'Malley for being able to do such a long and complex speech without hard copy or autocue. He was that good.

Harney never came near us and never used autocue. But she could handle a nuanced, detailed twenty-minute address without hesitation.

It's doubtful her equal was to be found in the last century. While every party, particularly the lawyer-ridden Fine Gael, has produced brilliant orators, none has produced one who could work without a script as she could.

In response to her request to meet me, Pádraig Flynn's secretary Gerry Rice and I went to her office, where she advanced the possibility that I might work with her as well as with the senior minister. It would, she said, obviate misunderstandings and help create a unified public presentation of the Department of the Environment. Gerry, who hadn't been invited to have an opinion, studiously regarded his hands. Having been an air-traffic controller in a previous incarnation, he knew when to talk and when not to talk.

When the minister of state finished, she looked at me from under her fringe in that way she does and waited. I said truthfully that I thought it would be wonderful and that I'd love it. Whether or not the minister would love it was outside of my control, but I thought it would be productive and also fun. The 'fun' bit seemed to throw her a little, but she bore it well. Gerry intervened to suggest that since the senior minister's view was pivotal to this happening, the next step must be for us to talk him through the proposition. 'Us' meant Gerry and me. It did not include Mary Harney. Mary and I considered this in silence, and, although neither of us articulated it, came to pretty much the same conclusion: the chances of Pádraig Flynn liking it would be improved by her absence from the discussion.

Gerry and I walked slowly back. A quintessential minister's office civil servant, Gerry was not going to share his opinion with me. We didn't discuss it as we went. Even so, by the time we arrived back in the dark corridor dominated by the minister's office, I'd have put down a bet that Gerry was convinced the dual-work proposal was not going to pass muster. Gerry knocked on the ministerial door and we were summoned inside. The minister instructed me to tell him what had happened. I did. He asked no questions, made no comment. After a long silence, he said he would not agree to the proposal, and that was it. Advisers advise and when, having given the argument their best shot, their advice is not taken, they either shut up or resign. I shut up and Gerry informed the minister of state that I would not be working for her.

I did work with her later, on several occasions, starting with the preparation for the Fair Deal Scheme and learned that you'd better have your ducks in a row before you engage with her because of the way she interrogates. She's one of those women, like Frances Fitzgerald, Helen McEntee and Máire Geoghegan-Quinn, who likes other women and pushes them into professional connection with each other. Today, the two of us are without any doubt that she continues to regard Pádraig Flynn with less than the affection I retain for him, but on this topic we give each other what thriller writer Robert B. Parker once described as 'a good leaving alone'.

Meanwhile, Tom would summon me, every now and then, for scriptwriting for the Taoiseach. The fact that I often knew little about the details of the policies reflected in the speeches didn't seem to matter. Or, rather, was an advantage. I didn't get entangled in the weeds, and anything I got wrong, Tom would instantly capture and fix. Sometimes, the notice was astonishingly short, as happened the day I came out of a training session in the company to be told that the Taoiseach's driver was in the lobby, ready to take me to Government Buildings, because Tom wanted something done. I took a notebook and got into the car, wondering if I should ask the Taoiseach's driver the reason for the summons. I decided against it, but while considering the possibility, met the driver's smiling eyes in the rear-view mirror.

'Great day,' he said.

It was lashing rain, so he clearly wasn't talking about the weather, but the news bulletin on the radio playing in the car didn't seem to suggest anything exceptional, so I nodded knowingly and shut up. Tom and Diggy met me at the door. Diggy always stood slightly behind Tom. Or maybe he stood slightly behind him when facing me because, I suspect, Diggy had a notion that I was dangerously volatile. On this occasion, Diggy was smiling like he'd never stop. Tom, on the other hand, was all business.

'Half an hour with the Taoiseach, then an hour, maybe an hour and a half, to write the piece to camera he's going to deliver tonight after the announcement of the ceasefire. Start with *qui bono*.'

With that, he knocked on the door of the Taoiseach's office, was shouted in, and there was Albert with the department secretary general and the minister for foreign affairs, all grinning like it was Christmas. The others buzzed off and I was left with the Taoiseach, a cup of tea each, and not a clue, other than *qui bono*.

'Okay, Taoiseach, you've practically no time, so let's get on with it,' I said, letting on to be in charge. 'Who gains most from this ceasefire?'

'The people who stand to gain most from it probably won't even know about it and they won't see the broadcast either. They're the children, North and South.' he told me. 'Our children. And grandchildren. They weren't around for the last twenty-five years of grief and tragedy. They don't know what a ceasefire can do. None of us does. But it will give them back their right to childhood.'

I was writing frantically, and when he stopped, glanced up to find the Taoiseach groping for a hanky to mop his tears.

'It will. It really will,' he told me. 'Whether they're on the Falls or the Shankill. Gives them the right that was stolen from generations.'

He went searching on his desk among the papers and produced a newspaper, flailing it at me to make me register the black and white photograph of a child of about six, perfectly groomed for the picture and his sibling, pop-eyed with babyhood. The two had been orphaned by a bomb. He talked about other atrocities and, trying to get him to some theme other than horror, I asked him some dumb question about how proud he was of the ceasefire. He lifted me out of it, telling me that nobody – neither individual nor group – 'owned' the ceasefire. But then he talked about something that had happened in his past that had changed him from being 'someone willing to work for peace, to someone obsessed by peace'. I asked him what that event was. It was an atrocity, was the answer, but he wasn't going to say any more than that. This speech wasn't about him. Well, to some degree it was, I said, asking what he wanted to say about Tánaiste Dick Spring, with whom

Albert had the kind of chaotic and occasionally venomous relationship that characterises coalitions, especially when the leader of one of the two parties is as impulsive and obstinate as Albert. He was generous about Spring and about John Hume.

A knock on the door presaged Tom's arrival with several senior civil servants. The audience was over. Recording was in three hours, which meant the script had to be written, cleared, timed and put on to the then Neanderthal system of autocue within the next two hours. I was led into a secretarial office and pointed at a word processor.

'You didn't record him?' Tom asked.

'Like I'd have the time to transcribe a recording.'

Tom left and from my notes and my recent memory of the pattern of Albert's thoughts and words, I crafted a lovely script. It was lovely because it was true. True to what he had said and what he was. When the autocue was set up in front of him, he read it through once, with Diggy, Tom and me braced for dispute. No dispute. Not a word to be changed. He looked up impatiently, indicated he was ready to go, and did it flawlessly. It went out that night and I watched it at home with Tom, agreeing with the Taoiseach's driver. It was a great, great day. One of the few days of unalloyed joy for Albert in the Taoiseach's office.

The next Albert outing was not a great day and it's one that reflects badly on me. I was thrilled to get the chance to script a piece to camera for him to deliver in what I think may have been a planned fireside chat from the Taoiseach's apartment. Arriving to direct the shoot, I was confident, because the script had been parsed and punished by Bart, Diggy, Tom, and several VIPs from the Department of the Taoiseach together with other departments like Foreign Affairs and had survived pretty much intact. We had a great autocue operator and cameraman, and although I didn't know the sound guy, he seemed coolly competent. Just as we were about to start filming, I asked Barry Kelly, a superb ex-RTÉ cameraman who had worked with Tom in Africa on a shoot for Gorta, if he'd let me look in the viewfinder so I'd know exactly what the viewer would eventually see. No problem. He shifted sideways and I stared at the tiny oblong, spotting that sitting behind Albert's shoulder was Alex Comfort's then-famous book *The Joy of Sex*. I climbed across flexes to remove it, which slightly irritated Albert. I explained that viewers, faced with laden bookshelves, are notorious for turning their heads sideways to read the titles of books and that this particular title just might present a little bit of a distraction.

I counted down, gave Albert the signal, and he false-started. The guys knew to keep the camera rolling, so the Taoiseach was given a signal – go again. In your own time. He got halfway through a paragraph and fell over a word. We stopped recording and I checked the word that had tripped him. No scriptwriter can afford to be pricklyproud in this situation. If the speaker stumbles over a word, it's the scriptwriter's job to come up with a better word. But Albert wanted no substitutes. He said nothing was wrong with the word, it was just a first run-through and we'd keep going. Barry Kelly glanced sideways at me and I solemnly told him the Taoiseach was right – let's just keep going, this was just a first run-through, but we'd record it in case we captured something really good. We all took a deep breath and off he went again. This time, when he stopped, he said the autocue was going too fast. The operator looked hurt. He had been varying the pace perfectly to match the Taoiseach's reading speed but immediately took the blame and promised to concentrate more. Oddly, the Taoiseach didn't seem mollified by this and began to query the lighting. Again, one of the crew got up and very obviously tinkered with one of the blond lights while leaving it more or less the same.

Albert then wanted to go back to the beginning, which suited us all, so we agreed that would be the best. When it came to the third sentence, he stumbled over the same word and gave out dog's abuse to me for not changing it. I suggested two options and he told me I was supposed to be able to write things; why was I asking him to do my job? I picked one of the words, it was inserted in the autocue, which was rolled back to the top and we started again, only for the new word to cause a problem. He started to complain and I cut across him, saying that I was going to cut this short, because it was taking up too much of the Taoiseach's valuable time, and since we faced no urgent deadline it could be tackled at some other, better time. Relieved, he got up and as the sound man took the microphone off him, talked about the problems as if we had created them. The crew began silently to de-rig as Albert went into another room. We didn't talk about what had happened, simply exchanging mystified glances. Each of us had been on shoots where a camera operator was as pissed as a newt or a sound man was easily distracted or a scriptwriter was precious in their protection of every word they had crafted. None of that applied in this instance, and none of us understood what we had just witnessed. The crew would get paid anyway and get home earlier than expected, so they gave a communal shrug and arranged to go to the nearest pub for a pint or two.

I headed for Government Buildings, where I encountered Seán Duignan and Tom in great humour, expecting me to tell them the shoot had been a wild success. I told them what had happened.

'I won't ever work with that man again,' I told them. 'I don't know what got into him, but it had fuck all to do with the script or the autocue or the direction.'

I was blind with rage and defensiveness, but also confused. Now, with the wisdom of hindsight, I can't help wonder if what happened was an early appearance of the Alzheimer's that blighted Albert's later years. Dementia doesn't manifest itself in an incrementally obvious way. In its early stages, it can appear in sudden, unrepeated visits. How Albert behaved was so out of kilter with his normal affable self, how he managed the script so at odds with his normal competence, that it might have been useful if the person in charge – me – had registered his behaviour and analysed it as indicative of an emerging problem. I might also have remembered Tom's earlier reproof of me, when he said Albert never retained certain communication principles Tom taught him. That may have been a consequence of an age-related diminution rather than a constant characteristic. (Nobody had ever, up to that point, accused Albert of not learning. He was a smart man who was more than able to develop and grow – up to the period when he became Taoiseach.) I am ashamed to say I didn't do any of that. I was more focused on him not appreciating a good script and taking direction from an expert. It was all about me.

I never encountered Albert again while he was Taoiseach. In fact, the only time I ever met him after that was when President Barack Obama and Michelle Obama came to Ireland and the then Taoiseach, Enda Kenny, invited me to be present when the US president met a small group in the old Bank of Ireland headquarters opposite Trinity. Albert was on the bus from Government Buildings as it crawled through the heavily guarded, blocked-off streets of the capital. I sat beside him and looked after him as best I could.

He was sweet and lost and trusting, asking the same question repeatedly, enthralled by the mounted gardaí in the streets. Like a child, he was willing to be minded and obedient to instructions, all the memories of what he had achieved and the lives he had saved gone.

15

HERE'S YOUR MARTELLO TOWER

When Dermot McCrum, the managing director of Carr Communications, asked how the shareholders would feel about a management buy-out, I said probably positively. Aidan Meade and Dominic McNamara had left the company, Aidan to set up his own consultancy, Dominic to become head of fundraising for Maynooth University, based in Chicago. I talked to Bunny and Tom. Bunny had retired and he and Joan were under increasing pressure because of post-polio syndrome, which was lessening Joan's physical capacities. They were going to need a lot more help and it would be expensive. So the answer to Dermot's question was going to be a yes. I asked Tom and Bunny to let me set the price and do the negotiations and they agreed. I set a high price and told Dermot that since he was managing director and had been in that job for several years, due diligence could hardly apply. They met the price and the company changed hands, with Tom and I tied to two-year work-out contracts. We were improbably rich for a brief period.

Then, one day, when I had just finished a training session, Tom arrived into my office.

'C'mon,' he said.

'C'mon where?'

'Never mind, just c'mon.'

I shrugged, herded stuff into a drawer, and followed him out the door and into the vintage Merc Anton had given him as a birthday present. He drove northwards but further north on the M1 than the Sutton/Howth exit, eventually taking the Skerries/Donabate/Portrane exit, which was okay with me because we had spent several summer holidays in Skerries when I was a child, near the stony, rather than the sandy, beach, so the associations were good. In this instance, however, Skerries did not materialise. Instead, we went through Donabate and took another long boring country road towards Portrane, where I had never been before. Eventually, Tom found an entrance largely concealed by hedges and drove through an open farm gate onto a long drive between irregular hedging on the right and what looked like Beirut after intense bombing on the left. The drive eventually turned to the right and the Merc did a semi-circle before coming to a halt beside a parked car.

'Here's your Martello,' Tom said, gesturing at the building in front of us.

Now, most Martello towers are ugly, but this was arguably the ugliest I had ever seen, with speckled stone on the outside and extensions stuck on, apparently at random, at some point in the past by someone who hated Martellos. A small young man emerged from the parked car and dithered in a positive way while the two of us gazed up at the building with a For Sale sign on it.

'You've always wanted a Martello,' Tom pointed out. 'Now we have the money to buy one. And look', he added, as if he had laid it on personally, 'a double rainbow.'

All Martellos were built, in the first years of the nineteenth century, to the same basic design, but each is unique. For example, the one on Ireland's Eye is bigger than most of the similar structures on the mainland, because island-based Martellos needed to support bigger cannons. All of them differ from the original tower in Corsica in having a 'machicolation', an extra structure sticking out over the main entrance with holes in it to allow boiling water or pitch to be poured down on anybody trying to get in. A variant on this warmly welcoming approach, the pitch cap, had, a few centuries earlier, been called 'caip bháis', giving rise to the expression 'to put the kibosh' on someone.

The Martello towers on the south side of Dublin are built of cut granite, whereas most of the ones on the northside are built of rough stone sourced locally and covered with render. Twenty-four towers were built around Dublin, because at the time – 1800 to 1806 – it was regarded as such a strategically important port. Each was built close enough to the next to ensure that the arc of the cannon on the roof of one would touch the arc of the cannon on the top of the next one – that way, ships wouldn't be able to sneak in between the towers.

As time went on, many of the Martellos, here and in the UK, became derelict. The RAF used some of the ones on the south coast of England for target practice at the outset of the Second World War. In Ireland, a couple fell into the sea. One on the southside was knocked down so a railway could be built through where it had been. But a few – maybe six or seven – came into private ownership in the late nineteenth and early twentieth centuries. Like the Joyce Tower on the southside. And Hicks Tower, the one between Portmarnock and Malahide, on which someone at some point put a conical roof, so few people appreciate that it is a Martello.

The second week after we moved in, Tom went for a walk, and, arriving at the green cottage at the corner, knocked. When its owner, Mary (or Moll) Lynders appeared, he greeted her in typical Tom terms.

'I'm your new next-door neighbour, Tom Savage,' he told her, extending a hand. 'Are you good for a cup of tea?'

Was she what? Mary Lynders is the kind of woman who always has scones on a wire cooler, fresh out of the oven, and the two of them became deep friends, right there. They talked for hours. About the tower, the history of the neighbourhood, her family and the various people who had lived in the Martello. About politics and policies and the history book she was reading. Mary Lynders read the *Irish Independent* from cover to cover every day and is one of the best-informed people around.

Eventually, Tom got up to go, suggesting that she must meet me at some point. She stopped dead.

'Is your wife a gardener?'

Tom, laughing at the very idea, shook his head.

'Are *you* a gardener?'

Another head shake. Her face lit up. In that case, she told him, she would be up the following day to tell him (and me) all about the garden, which had been cared for by her husband for years before his death. The following day, there she was, headscarf on and cigarette on her lower lip, ordering the two of us to examine this bit of the garden and be outraged at the condition of that bit. I brought out cups of tea and herself and Tom sat on a low wall, talking as if they'd been friends for decades. Before she left, she pulled away shrubs to show us historic mile markers – two of them – she had essentially concealed from some previous owners she didn't think deserved to know about them. The concealment was achieved by growing shrubs up around them.

Moll Lynders sums up her background as having been, at seventeen, in a reference to 'Ruby in the kitchen', working as a domestic servant-in-training for a surgeon's family. The reference is to *The Forsyte Saga*. Or perhaps *Upstairs, Downstairs*.

> Ruby carried the firewood up the stairs and put a fire in all the drawing rooms and peeled the potatoes or swept the floors. When you were Ruby in the kitchen, you did what the cook told you to do and that was that. Well, you didn't know a whole lot, so you were glad to have a job really. And to be taught something. We had only an open fire and a pot oven, that's how my mother cooked and baked. It's a bar put across an open fire and a three-legged iron pot with two lugs on each side and you baked your bread in that. If you were lucky enough, you'd have turf, and turf would smoulder and keep the lid hot on the top of your pot and the fire baked your bread underneath.

Later, she worked as a nurse in St Ita's Hospital, and became the local go-to person in emergencies, even when those emergencies had the potential to be life-changing.

I was off this one day and there was this young chap, thirteen, snaggin' turnips with a knife and he took his thumb off and my brother brought him over to me. So I washed it with Dettol until I got all the clay out of it. There was no motor cars and no doctor in Donabate. The nearest doctor was in Swords and he might have a bike and that was it. You wouldn't get to Temple Street Hospital. So I stitched the youngster's thumb and every time he'd see a bit of blood he would faint. But he didn't lose his thumb.

Mary Lynders is a walking oral history, not just of growing up in the forties and fifties, but of the area surrounding our Martello. Rural electrification reached Donabate in 1946, she told us, remembering it vividly. 'We got the power and they only did two rooms and the kitchen and one plug for an electric kettle, you weren't allowed have another one. And if you could afford it you could rent the cooker from the ESB. You couldn't buy an electric cooker, they rented them out to you.'

With Mary's help, we spent a year finding out what was where in the Martello. Because some previous owner had hated any exposed stone, everything was covered with plasterboard, and false ceilings concealed not just the barrel vault, but virtually everything overhead. Imagining what had been there was difficult. Imagining what to replace that with was even more daunting, despite the clarity given to the project by architect Sue Casey's drawings. On the other hand, we were learning more about Martello towers in general, occasionally thinking of the tower in Cork which was used to store gunpowder during the Civil War. A spark exploded the whole lot of it, but the outer walls and the roof held. Which made it much easier to refurbish later. During the year we refurbished our tower, we frequently envied the owners of that tower their much simpler task, although we did have, for free, the services of Anton, who I suspect is now the greatest living expert in this architectural defence oddity.

On St Patrick's Day, that first year when we lived in the tower, Anton rang first thing in the morning.

'Ma, can I come round and punch a hole in one of your ceilings?'

Since all the ceilings were going to be taken down within a matter of months, this didn't seem that outrageous a request, so I said that would be okay, just asking why the ceiling-punching fancy had taken him.

'I think I've worked out where the intramural space is that allowed them to pull the cannonballs to the roof.'

He came, drilled a ring of holes in the ceiling, punched a fist through and there it was exactly as it had been when a previous owner decided it was without merit and that they would cover it up. Bricked partway with a rusted iron hoop through which the chain pulley would have run.

Much the same thing happened when the company that was disassembling the tower attacked the kitchen. Tom and I had moved to the Rocket House at that point. We were there for a year, and one bleak year it was, in a tiny unheated building without insulation. We consoled ourselves by imagining how beautiful the tower would be when it was refurbished, although visiting it during the long transformation process was often interesting while not necessarily encouraging. The removal of all the plasterboard left us facing masonry, rather than stones, and so a shot blaster had to be hired to shoot a million tiny black bullets at the wall in order to peel off the dirty-grey coating. The shot-blaster worked in half-hour stretches. After thirty minutes, health and safety rules dictated that the operator abandon the black-fogged atmosphere within the tower and spend half an hour in the open air. It seemed particularly Irish that he whiled away these half-hours smoking a cigarette. When he was done and the deep floor covering of miniature bullets and dust had been hoovered up, the stonework was revealed as it had not been for more than a hundred years: big, beautiful, uneven bluish stone, from a now defunct quarry in Skerries, placed with mathematical precision to create massy solid defensive walls.

It was after that the kitchen units were removed from the narrow galley area they had occupied, and it was Anton who said to one of the team, 'Bryan, you know how there should be a spiral staircase coming down to this floor, but there isn't? I think they bricked the spiral staircase into this wall. When you have the kitchen units pulled off the wall, would you have a go with a Kango hammer at this wall and see if you can find the spiral staircase?'

That's what happened, and three days later, Bryan sent a text that said 'I have found the spiral staircase. I feel like Indiana effing Jones!' Walter Douglas's workmen, having breached the wall through which the spiral staircase wound its way, had then cut away the lower steps, thrown them into the void and just cemented the whole lot together. We laid the recovered steps out in order and asked Fionnuala Maye, then the Heritage Architect at Fingal County Council, who herself had transformed a Martello in Howth into a radio museum, to come and look at what we'd found. She took one look and shook her head. No reconstruction. Everything the Savages did to the tower had to be clearly different from the rest, clearly identifiable as done during the early years of the twenty-first century. We might not agree with those rules – and, time and again as we reconstructed the Martello tower, we found we seriously disagreed with some of them – but if the rules said no reconstruction, no reconstruction would happen. The old steps were stored and a new end put to the spiral staircase in iron and wood by the late David Sheane, who built the Formula Sheane racing cars in which Anton had been a champion driver.

Joe Ryan, MD of Hanley Pepper, the structural engineers, worried aloud for days on end about the task of ensuring that the first floor was structurally sound and the roof wouldn't fall in. Sue Casey was worrier-in-chief. Although in real life Sue is the sort of funny and buoyant personality you desperately want to find yourself sitting beside at an event that promises to be boring, on this project she worried for Ireland. Nothing was too small for her to agonise over. Fingal County

Council liked her because she never left a detail undealt with. Everybody working on the tower liked her because she didn't make like the important architect she was, and, because she worried so concentratedly, pulled together to make sure everything was done the way she wanted it done. (Sue gave up architecture after this project, and I have always guiltily wondered if our Martello killed her interest.)

Everything cost three times as much as the original estimates, so halfway through, even though we had borrowed a fortune from Ulster Bank and my sister had lent me all she possessed, I began to worry that we might never get the place complete enough to live in. But then I would climb the spiral staircase – so narrow, so confined, because it had been built by and for the products of the British slums of the time; little underfed guys withered by constant cigarette smoking – and I would decide to keep going, even if it meant a bigger debt for longer. The idea of living in a tower that had once held sixteen 'invalided' soldiers – men stumping around on peg-legs following a war injury – enthralled me, as Tom had known it would. And the continuum of new information was fascinating, too. One of the unique features of this tower is that it has a double machicolation. It took us a long time to work out that it had been added in the 1930s to keep the symmetry with the roof of the room inserted below.

The kitchen was effectively given to me by a lovely man named Kieran Lyons. Kieran I first met when he was a journalist interviewing me for some magazine. I liked him tremendously, and a couple of years later contacted him to ask what he was doing and if he was okay. It turned out that he had left his job to take care of his dying mother. We met up a number of times, became close friends, and collaborated together on a book for Chartered Accountants Ireland entitled *This Business of Writing*. We had talked about making a dream kitchen in the tower and he had promised he would visit and genuinely eat a meal, as opposed to the fastidious picking he usually did, but that never happened, because his life became too much for him and he left it. But not before he wrote a will leaving enough money to a handful of friends to make a life-changing difference to each. I got my dream kitchen, and every time I walk into it I think of him and thank him.

A few weeks after we trekked back from the Rocket House, I arrived home from work to find a stranger cleaning the windows from the outside with newspapers and vinegar. When he turned around, I realised he had been one of the crew from the company that had done the bulk of the work. That company had since gone under, in the face of the Anglo disaster and wider financial recession. Bryan, I thought. Bryan Greene.

'It's all right,' he said, as I got out of the car. 'You don't have to pay me.'

'Sorry? Did Tom ask you to clean the windows?'

Nobody had asked him. He had fallen in love with the tower during the long project, and figured that because of sea spray, we would need the windows washed. We had a cup of coffee and identified a couple of other things that needed doing. But because at this point Ulster Bank were being dictatorial about how much I would pay them back each week, I was not sure I'd be able to pay him the going rate. Whatever the going rate was. He said we'd manage.

About a week later, when I came home, I found him, Tom and Mary Lynders in the driveway, Bryan and Mary smoking, Tom clutching a cup of tea. Mary told me I needed weeding and gardening and she was going to teach Bryan how to do both. Tom did a 'don't blame me' shrug behind her and when she turned away, Bryan did exactly the same. All I could do was laugh and surrender. In the following couple of years, Mary taught Bryan Greene to be a superb gardener and passionate with it. At first, they worked side by side, with her teaching him the Latin names of every plant.

When Mary got cancer a few years ago, Tom and I and Bryan were heart-struck. Bryan continued to take care of the acre of varied plants on his own, and she would ring him and demand he drive her down for an inspection. She managed cancer the same way she managed everything else; beat it into being a chronic rather than an immediately fatal disease, and dealt with the pain with the same impatient effectiveness. It didn't stop her scene-stealing when her two daughters featured in an episode of Dermot Bannon's *Room to Improve*. The programme director, Linda Cullen, knew she had two big personalities in the two daughters, but their mother was out on her own, and the reaction to her when the programme was broadcast was phenomenal.

One of the things Revenue do for you, if you own an old house, is designate as tax-free any money you spend on keeping it standing and not rotting, as long as you open the building to the public about sixty days of the year. Hence the framed notice outside our tower, telling passersby a little about it and inviting them to join one of the tours taking place on Saturdays and Sundays throughout the summer. Pandemic summer in 2020 was the exception, and it felt strange, on warm weekend mornings, not to be doing a frantic clean and tidy so that at nine o'clock I could stand in front of a group and begin: 'The Martello towers of Britain and Ireland were arguably the biggest mistake ever made by the British Admiralty ...' Bryan does the upstairs and roof part of the tour except when a project takes him away for a weekend.

In the few years before Tom's death, he would let on to be irritated at the invasion as I led people into the round room where he sat in a big leather chair in front of the woodburning stove. Since Bryan and I did the heavy lifting, the only thing that really bothered Captain Sport, Anton's nickname for his father, was that he couldn't watch matches while a tour was happening. Instead, he would read the sports pages of the *Irish Times*, *Irish Independent* and *Irish Examiner*, one after another. Invariably, though, when one of the visitors asked me a question, he would look across and say, 'That's a Tyrone accent' or 'Which part of Cavan are you from?' And the individual addressed would nip over, sit down beside him and within minutes the two of them would be listing off mutual friends and acquaintances. Tom knew someone from everywhere, and half the time, the week after the tour, he'd get letters or emails from the people he'd talked with.

The work on the tower happened during our two-year work-out with the consortium that had bought our company. My friend Alan

Crosbie, who had written a book about family businesses, warned me against work-outs, which he said never worked. I ignored him. Pity. They were two unpleasant years. But once we were free to move, we did, and Anton came up with a debt-free structure for our new venture, The Communications Clinic. Because we were enjoined against poaching any existing staff, we not only didn't, but ran a newspaper ad promising that whoever we picked to join our staff would probably be paid *less* than what they were on, because we wanted workaholics who just loved working on communications and learning about this ever-evolving field. Several of our former colleagues took the pay cut to join us and create a success in the teeth of a recession.

This time, thanks to Anton, we never went through the baptism of fire offered by loss-making years. The Communications Clinic was profitable from the first year and we were back to having fun doing what we loved with people we liked working with.

16

When Politicians Fall Out with One Another

My life never joined up. I was a woman running a communications consultancy or retained by cabinet ministers to advise them. I was also a novelist and non-fiction writer, producing, on average, one book every two years from the time I was twenty-six. I didn't always agree with what one publisher did with my work – being changed into Terri in order to attract more female readers I thought crazy and still do – but I was lucky in that Mercier Press showed amazing faith in me from early on and sold rights to my novels all over Europe. I was lucky, too, that my first editor, Jo O'Donoghue, an author herself, kept me clamped to her side as she moved between publishers and set up her own imprint. Jo has an eidetic memory for text and was able to prevent me plagiarising myself.

What I mean about my life not joining up is that the people who knew me for communications advice were rarely the people who read my novels. Of course, politicians, as a group, tend not to be readers, with the notable exceptions of retired Minister for Finance Michael Noonan and current Minister for Public Expenditure and Reform Paschal Donohoe.

Once, when I worked for Pádraig Flynn, the department secretary general contacted me to tell me he had changed a speech I wrote for the minister. One of the ministerial rules was that this should not happen. In this case, the senior man explained, the minister had been called away and a minister of state had substituted for him. The section of the speech where the minister spoke of a book he had read had been deleted. I didn't care one way or another, but pointed out that I always phrased quotes from books so the person delivering the speech didn't have to have read the particular book. Oh, he accepted that, the secretary general said. It wasn't that the minister of state wouldn't have read this particular book. It was that if it sounded like he was claiming to ever have read *any* book, it would provoke laughter.

My novel-writing habit was either not known to many of the politicians who knew me, or was regarded as a marginally threatening personal eccentricity, evoking the classic 'I don't want to be in your next book' from TDs who were too dull to be put in any book, as testified to by the hard work represented by reading their own election leaflets.

Another place where the pieces don't join up is where two political clients fall out with each other. If you were no part of the break-up, then, logically, you should be able to continue to be friends with each side. But it can mirror what happens when a couple you've known since they were teenagers split up. Staying loyal to both is always seen by one of them as deeply disloyal.

Sometimes you're present when the falling-out happens. The most vivid example of that for me was when someone came into the boardroom in Fine Gael headquarters (across the road a bit from the Fianna Fáil equivalent) to say that Frank Flannery was on *Morning Ireland* and would the Leader like to hear the programme? Enda Kenny nodded, someone pushed a button and Frank Flannery's high voice filled the room. Flannery, together with General Secretary Tom Curran, had travelled the length and breadth of the country as part of a reconfiguration of the party which had been markedly successful. Now, though, he was being asked about future coalitions involving Fine Gael, and stating, with comfort and confidence, that the party might have no choice but to go into partnership with Sinn Féin.

Up to then, I had seen Enda Kenny in merry joke-telling mode. I had seen him in gentle listening mode. I had seen him in serious oratorical mode. I had never seen him in full-on rage mode and even one glance at him made me grateful I wasn't Flannery. Their relationship changed utterly in that moment. Party officials were told to brief journalists to the effect that such a partnership would never happen as long as Mr Kenny was leader. As I remember it, nothing was added to that blunt cut-off. I have no idea if the two men talked thereafter, but, other than courteous mutual acknowledgements at the funerals of mutual friends, I doubt it.

Many, if not most, companies hired by political parties are employed, at least in part, because they overtly share the politics of their employer. My companies always made it clear that our political beliefs were our own business and no part of our marketing. That said, it frequently irked politicians with whom we had worked to find us working with another party, as we did, down the years, serving people from Labour, the Progressive Democrats and the Green Party. When they raised it with us, we would explain that we were always open to a retainer that prevented us from sharing our genius with their competitors.

In the early days, the Green Party was a particular delight to work with, because they weren't like a political party at all. They carried no baggage, were dogged by no scandal. They had also never experienced the full viciousness of politics and, most important, had never experienced defeat. I did several media training courses with them, meeting the young Eamon Ryan, who later appointed Tom Savage to run the RTÉ Authority. The party had a honeymoon second only to that of the Progressive Democrats, but experienced periods in government that cut the legs from under them more radically than happened the PDs.

It was Charlie Haughey who took Fianna Fáil into coalition, a move many of his colleagues saw as a shocking assault on the party's 'core values'. They all knew it for what it was: a surrender of majority rule.

That was what made it so painful to many of them; knowing that it said, effectively, that Fianna Fáil would never again be in government on its own. When this was expressed to Tom, he scoffed. Charlie Haughey had solved the problems of Fianna Fáil for the following twenty years, he told them. The party was on a decline anyway. A decided, if slow, decline. By going into coalition, Haughey had created a precedent that – if Fianna Fáil played their cards right – would have them in power for most, if not all, of the next period. They could go into coalition with Labour, the Progressive Democrats or the Greens. (Nobody then could imagine a coalition between Fianna Fáil and Fine Gael.)

Fianna Fáil took a while to adapt to the new normal and drove some of their coalition partners, most notably Labour, crazy with behaviour drawn from their lone-party-in-government days. What nobody could have anticipated was that while the gradual decline of Fianna Fáil would continue, most of the parties with which they sequentially shared power suffered a much steeper decline that led to them being crushed at the followed general election with – as just one example – the Greens retaining just one seat in the 2024 contest.

During the early months of Albert Reynolds' administration, I was too busy to notice what was going on with Bertie Ahern. Indeed, not many people noticed what he was doing, which wasn't much. He was a minister but not a prominent one. Eventually, I registered that he was wandering around the corridors of power like a spavined donkey, looking depressed. I rang him and suggested we have breakfast in the Shelbourne, just a short walk from Leinster House or Government Buildings, one of which would be his post-breakfast destination.

I was seated at the table when Bertie sloped in. No other way to describe it. It was a slope. He was, as he always is, friendly to the waiting staff and to me, but it was still a slope. This was not a happy man. As soon as we had ordered, I asked him what was eating him. This so obviously surprised him that I realised he had an agenda in mind and this wasn't it. I fished around a bit and found that Bertie seemed to think that I was there to look for his forgiveness related to the bringing down of Haughey. His point seemed to be that all was fair in war and leadership contests, and that, all credit to me, I had arranged it very cleverly, the way I had put out Flynn the previous Sunday to set it all up for Doherty. Before I could get my head around that, he told me he also didn't hold against Tom the line about where he, Bertie, lived. I was completely confused and grateful for the distraction of the food arriving. (I was, of course, delighted with the food itself, but it did serve a dual purpose that morning.)

I asked Bertie to go back to the beginning of what he had said and he repeated it. Fascinating, to see a series of accidents woven into a clever plot. Okay, I said, first things first. It was Vincent Browne who had contacted, not me, but Pádraig Flynn the week before. It was Vincent who sensed that Haughey was losing ground that mattered with the firing of the Country & Western Alliance. It was Vincent who wanted Flynn to give him a substantial piece for the *Sunday Tribune*. Now, fair enough, Flynn grasped the opportunity with both hands; why wouldn't he? Fair enough, also, I had recorded and transcribed Flynn's words, ordered the paragraphs and made sure that what went to Vincent was usable. That RTÉ liked what they read that Sunday, and put Flynn on the lunchtime news, was a consequence of the editor of the *Turbine* (as hacks called it) putting Flynn on the front page and giving his essay a full inside page.

I could see that Bertie only half-believed me. A good conspiracy is stickier than superglue, and from Bertie's position, the logic of 'putting out Flynn' the week before Doherty blew was inescapable. I pointed out that Albert didn't want Doherty to do what he did and put up a good fight to prevent it, but while Bertie was prepared – reluctantly – to accept that I had not orchestrated a fortnight of cleverality, and although I pointed without detail to the promotion of Dr John O'Connell as interesting in that context (without the detail I had about John's motivation, which was none of Bertie's business), the conspiracy theory might have been dented, but it was still there, as we found out when Justin O'Brien's book about Haughey emerged. In it, Bertie told him he didn't know who 'set up' Doherty's apology but credited Albert

Reynolds and Pádraig Flynn with advance knowledge neither actually had. He half-believed Albert, as well, bitterly dismissing the prospect of the Taoiseach delivering on his departure date. According to his autobiography, Albert 'had already given [Bertie] my word that my stay would be a limited one, at the most six years, and that when he was ready I would support him as the one to take over as leader.' In his book, Albert described Bertie as 'happy to wait.' The man sitting across from me in the Shelbourne was anything but happy about his lot. He believed that once Albert got the habit of power, he would want to stay for longer than six years.

'You may be right,' I said, 'but Albert's not going to be in power for anything like six years.'

Bertie looked at me, eyes narrowing with the internal question *How does she know this?*

'I'm just telling you,' I said, with no clue as to how I knew so categorically. 'He'll be in power for less than half that time. You'll get your chance much sooner than you expect, and you need to get your act together and start looking like a future leader.'

I specified a number of behaviours to be amended and – as he always did in response to any advice from anyone – Bertie nodded appreciatively. He would decide later if he'd go along with anything I was suggesting, although, as a kicker, I pointed out to him that I had nothing to gain by telling him to fly straight. One way or the other, when Albert's leadership collapsed, Bertie was ready to succeed.

Bertie's communication style has led to much mocking media coverage and even a few small books. But the former leader of Fianna Fáil can, when he wants to, communicate with absolute lucidity. Anyone hearing him in recent years as a political commentator on national media can testify to that. The first time I saw him at his communicative best was when he did an hour on canvassing at a course we were running for Fianna Fáil candidates coming up to a general election. It was breathtaking. The participants started off smiling and nodding and then got serious, making notes as fast as they could. They were in no doubt that this was high priority, or why. The way Bertie talked about each encounter with a constituent made them realise that it was an opportunity to stamp their individual and party brand on that constituent's brain. Not that he even mentioned branding. It was a presentation rooted in respect for the voter and a visceral understanding of how to build relationships with voters. Bertie, a man it was easy to believe had been born with what James Madison called the 'little arts of popularity,' shrugged off that myth. Those little arts were at anybody's disposal if they stopped admiring themselves and concentrated their attention on other people. He was also blunt about arguing with people encountered on the street, knowing that new candidates were too often eager to be seen – especially in the eyes of any media present – as experts and well able for the gobshites they might meet on the doorsteps. None of the participants believed that when Bertie finished, and they had run smack into a reality many of them had missed up to this point, which is that if you defeat someone in an argument on their own doorstep in front of witnesses, the chances of them later voting for you might be somewhat reduced.

The other person who is startlingly impressive at seminars, particularly seminars designed to increase the parliamentary representation of women, is Frances Fitzgerald, one of my heroes. The night before she resigned as Tánaiste and Minister for Justice on 28 November 2017, Frances came to my house, the two of us sitting in the glow of a woodburning stove while I failed to dissuade her from her planned resignation. She was innocent – and later to be adjudged innocent in a judicial investigation – but that didn't matter, she told me. If she continued in role while continuing to fight the constant accusations, it would damage Fine Gael, and she was never going to do that.

The resignation was courageous and seen as that by the electorate who sent her off to Europe afterwards, where she continued to fight for the issues, explicitly those involving or damaging women, for which she had fought since her days as a social worker. Her post-Oireachtas career has been an object lesson in resilience and recovery. But it's worth pointing out that the two highest-placed women in Ireland at that time, Frances Fitzgerald and Nóirín O'Sullivan, the first female

Garda commissioner in the nearly century-long history of the force, were simultaneously wrongly hounded out of office. O'Sullivan was also found innocent of the charges laid against her. Leo Varadkar should have fought for Frances. Instead, he defined her as someone who, in an ideal world, would be fought for, while sending a senior civil servant to Nóirín when she was on her summer break, to suggest she take a hike, on the basis that there was 'too much noise' around her. The former Garda commissioner took her bruised self off to New York to become UN Assistant Secretary-General for the Department of Safety and Security. Having rebuilt her career and having had her reputation handed back to her by a judge, in May 2023 she was appointed by the Ceann Comhairle to chair a taskforce on safe participation in political life, a hugely relevant issue, given the threats to the life and family of Minister Helen McEntee, who bore them – and the home evacuation they caused – with a characteristically quiet courage that should never have been asked of her.

17

Sure They're All the Same

The election count is going on all over the country, and RTÉ radio and TV has a rolling programme with commentators swapping seats and cutaways to count centres and recently elected TDs, along with those unfortunates due to put the word 'former' before their title, talking on camera.

Michael Healy-Rae, the one with the cap, is on screen, talking almost medieval prose. Glancing away from the monitor, I intercept knowing glances between the presenter and other panellists: Sure isn't he a character, all the same? You have to hand it to those Healy-Raes. The tiny mutual smirks are typical of the national media when it comes to the two South Kerry TDs. You'd have to be courteous in your questioning, all right, but that section of your programme might have a flavour of low comedy about it.

That attitude is strange. It never strikes media interviewers and commentators who engage in this mental put-down that the Healy-Raes could – and do – run rings around them. In any given year, the two of them make more money in ventures outside politics than any of the eminences in the studios. Just one of Michael Healy-Rae's many companies, in June of 2025, was revealed to have made in the region of €840,000 in profit over the past two years. These guys are smart.

Business smart. Politics smart. Media smart. Not only are they smart, they could, in the old phrase, 'buy and sell' most of their media interlocutors, who are often so distracted by the caricature they represent that they do not notice the buying and the selling. Michael, particularly, has an acute sense of his media rights, recently telling one presenter – just before cutting off his phone – that if they weren't prepared to listen to his answers, and if they preferred to listen to themselves asking long questions, more power to them.

The way the Healy-Raes are treated in the national media always reminds me of the recurring whinge Fianna Fáil used to articulate when we first started to work with them. Interviewers treated them differently from Fine Gael or Labour, they claimed, because media favoured both over Fianna Fáil and particularly approved of Labour. Back then, this was a song to which we paid no attention whatever. It was ridiculous nonsense, all this blather about 'Dublin 4' thinking, like Mrs Doyle in *Father Ted* with her repeated instruction to have a cup of tea.

The last few years should have made us all revisit the 'Dublin 4' accusation, with its implication that many household-name print and broadcast journalists operate from a mindset and set of values not shared throughout the country. The classic example of this is Michael Lowry. National media takes a view of Lowry drawn from the tribunal that looked at money he received – a minister at the time making major decisions about mobile phone licences – from businesses not unrelated to the tender involved. If the national view of Lowry were shared by his electorate, he would have been out of politics long ago. The facts are otherwise. He tops the poll in his Tipperary North constituency and when the most recent government was being put together, led the Independents in their negotiations. A photograph of him giving the finger to critics in the Dáil chamber has been run again and again, and no evidence has ever surfaced that his local constituents regard it as anything other than a show of strength, and to hell with anybody who disapproved. Lowry doesn't need national media and he makes that clear.

Preparing people for media over five decades has obviously given me experience of different attitudes on the part of interviewers. Back in the day, the main RTÉ TV interviewer was Dr Brian Farrell, an academic who managed to probe, rather than perform. As time went on, however, the repeated mantra of 'I'm the one who asks the tough questions' was heard from RTÉ personalities, despite the patent idiocy of the claim. Asking tough questions is beside the point. All that matters is the answers. Listening and pursuing so that the answers are delivered are actually the relevant skills, and the first of those is unevenly distributed. Few broadcasters are good listeners. They're too eager to get centre-stage themselves, and when an answer is complex, as answers can necessarily be, they too often cut across it with an interruption.

It is a strange thing. In Ireland, we do market research into politicians, individually and severally, all the time. Up to our armpits, we are, in opinion polls. But we don't do opinion polls of journalists. That's not true of the United States, where outlets – before social media tightened budgets – used to anonymously poll journalists to find out their political loyalties. Journalists, in sometimes large percentages in the US, favour liberal or progressive politics. The likelihood is that this would be mirrored in Ireland, although we let on that all interviewers are born balanced and unbiased. We gloss over the increasingly used travel route whereby journalists move seamlessly from being unbiased interrogators into advisers to those they recently interrogated. I would love to see some university student doing research for a thesis examining the behaviour of broadcast journalists, because I believe that in some cases, it would be possible for a non-partisan listener, within ten seconds, to work out if the interviewee being questioned is an ordinary human being or a politician. It's dead easy, if you happen to turn on your car radio in the middle of a question, to work out, *simply by their tone of voice*, that it's a politician who is across the studio table.

That is stereotyping. It's making an inference that because someone is a public representative, and particularly if they are a government party TD, they are likely to deserve mistrust, contempt and derision.

That's not good for democracy. You cannot stop members of the general public saying the usual tripe about politicians:

They're all the same – out for themselves.

They all make promises they have no intention of keeping.

They all talk out of both sides of their mouths.

You never see them, after an election, until the next election is called.

It's a comfort to voters to sound knowing by making those statements in vox pop packages. (Those packages are the filler material that allows you to go and make a cup of coffee while missing nothing significant on the programme.) But it's questionable that radio and TV interviewers should make the same beliefs plain. Not all of them do it, and some past current affairs stars, such as Seán O'Rourke, never needed to do it. But a definite fashion is now in play that dictates that the broadcaster, to be regarded as fearless in the face of potential corruption, must look cynical (the single raised eyebrow trick), interrupt continuously, and adopt a quick-fire interrogative tone inviting the listener to believe the interviewee is guilty until proven innocent. I'm not complaining about this from the point of view of a trainer – any good trainer can equip their man or woman to survive and succeed in the face of this treatment – but I am suggesting that it is not a positive direction for public discourse, even if it gives the broadcaster a satisfying reputation.

It may, however, be inevitable, given what we know of opinion-forming on social media. Social media users react positively and approvingly to anger, abuse and debating put-downs. The feedback is persistent and the inference to be drawn by mainstream or legacy interviewers inescapable. If you want to be popular, if you want to be a household name, you need to hit hostility high doh with any politician the minute they appear before you, because you know, as day follows night, that this is the way to go. Particularly coming up to elections, the search is always on for the 'gotcha' question and the commentary is always about whether or not the presenter (or other candidate) found the 'smoking gun'. Business interviewers don't set out to land the gotcha question. Rather the reverse. Is it legitimate to behave as if politicians, as a profession, as a group, are venal, corrupt and incapable of giving honest answers to honest questions? Voters, here and in America, seem to come to more complex judgements about their politicians, opting in some cases to acknowledge bad behaviour but incorporating it into a wider assessment they make of that politician.

Media – and, indeed, academics – miss fascinating aspects of politics. Take, for instance, the situation Fine Gael asked me to take a look at during one general election campaign when the leader was the brainy John Bruton. Someone on the campaign team asked me if I'd have a look at the election bus dynamic, because they weren't sure it was working. 'The what?' The answer was impatient: 'Just have a look, would you?'

I got myself to one of the towns the bus was due to visit and found an observation post. The bus duly drew up and John Bruton got out. Then an extraordinary thing happened. Bruton stood for a moment while he selected the direction in which he should walk, and set off. The extraordinary thing was that people further down that street crossed the road to avoid the possibility of engaging with him. Unlike a fair few political figures of the time, Bruton was not crooked or corrupt. He was principled, committed, courteous and clever. But people simply didn't want to engage with him. Yet if you put Enda Kenny out in the same street, people would walk across the road *to* him. I recently watched Enda Kenny and his wife walking on a summer evening in Dublin, and literally every twenty paces they were stopped by strangers who wanted to engage. This was long after Kenny left power. But he gave them the free gift of his attention as if they were the most important thing – the most interesting thing – that had happened to him that day and often took out his little pad to make notes of what they were saying. Of most significance were the physicals. They stood close to him and they touched him. Shook hands with him. Took hold of his elbow. Mock-punched him in the upper arm.

Part of that was delight, a trait obvious in Kenny, missing in Bruton. Kenny takes delight in people. He loves skitting with them, mimicking them (Pádraig Flynn maintains that Kenny's imitation of Flynn is too squeaky). He takes delight in learning new things. He takes delight in his family. He takes delight in yarn-telling. He takes delight in a pint. He takes delight in physical activities. He is simply delighted with every day of his life. His delight is so contagious, people almost want to hold their hands out to warm their palms at the glow.

He's exceptional, too, in leaving the current party leader, Simon Harris, the hell alone. He doesn't give interviews or write columns advising the Tanaiste. He spotted Harris's potential when the latter was a very young politician, valued him — and now watches him in helpful silence.

Enda Kenny has always been an exceptional politician. His delight in people is not glad-handing. When he was party leader, he would often come from Brussels, fly into Dublin airport late in the evening and direct his driver to the home of a former colleague suffering a lingering terminal illness. He would arrive at their home, get launched into story-telling, make them laugh and then get into his car for the remainder of his journey to Mayo. Nobody knew about it, but that's the kind of thing he did and does. His concept of community service and of being useful to individuals did not stop when he left politics.

None of which precisely answers the question of how some people attract strangers to talk to them and others have to undergo remedial teaching so that they learn to keep their eyes on the person to whom they're talking, rather than looking over their shoulders to see if someone more interesting is coming along. Remedial communications training can go only so far. That said, the prospective candidate who larks and has fun with voters is a hell of a lot more likely to succeed over the long haul than the one who wants to tell them about his or her soaring vision. The one who enjoys the political process is more likely to survive, long term, than the one who wants to tell you about their miseries, real though those miseries may be.

The other politicians who succeed over many elections are the ones who cop on to the importance of a great team. Like Patrick O'Donovan, who figures – based on the number of people present at his thank-you night after an election – that his team is made up of about 200 people, a mixture of Fine Gael members, friends and family members.

'It includes poster people, canvassers, leaflet droppers and drivers', he says. 'People volunteer. A load of GAA people, for example, whose clubs I'd helped. Or people who might have got help from my constituency office and volunteered.'

That is the beauty of specifically Irish politics. It's local and it pulls people away from their social media-fuelled loneliness, creating a community of volunteers who believe in their man or their woman. Being part of such a team is hugely rewarding and ensures that the candidate stays rooted in local realities.

People who go into politics for money or power have a problem in Ireland. Neither is all that available. Even bribery is not the lively market it would have been twenty-five years ago, and the old rewards to the faithful, like membership of state boards, do not happen in the way they used to. Despite which, and despite trolling on social media, the supply of women and men eager to submit themselves to the judgement of the people seems endless, and – in my experience – the majority of them are hardworking, professional, interesting and fun.

BIBLIOGRAPHY

The Instant Tree
Bunny Carr
Mercier Press, 1975

Trivializing America: The Triumph of Mediocrity
Norman Corwin
Lyle Stewart, 1986

Bare Knuckles and Back Rooms: My Life in American Politics
Ed Rollins
Crown, 1997

Jiving at the Crossroads
John Waters
Blackstaff Press, 1991

The Boss: Charles J. Haughey in Government
Joe Joyce and Peter Murtagh
Poolbeg, 1993

All or Nothing: How Trump Recaptured America
Michael Wolff
Omnibus Press, 2023

Bibliography

The Splendid and the Vile: A Saga of Churchill, Family and Defiance During the Blitz
Erik Larson
Crown, 2020

My Autobiography
Albert Reynolds
Transworld, 2010

A Man for All Seasons
Robert Bolt
Heinemann and Bloomsbury Methuen Drama, 1960

Write and Get Paid for It
Terry Prone
Londubh, 2010

One Spin on the Merry-Go-Round
Seán Duignan
Blackwater Press, 1995

The Spy and the Traitor: The Greatest Espionage Story of the Cold War
Ben Macintyre
Penguin/Random House, 2018

The Modern Prince: Charles J. Haughey and the Quest for Power
Justin O'Brien
Merlin Publishing, 2002

INDEX

Ahern, Bertie, 54, 115, 116, 168–71
Ahern, Dermot, 119
AIDS, 84
Ailes, Roger, 71–2
Ainsworth, Joe, 103
air crew uniforms, 36–7
All or Nothing (Wolff), 69
Apprentice, The (BBC), 34
Arnold, Bruce, 98, 103
Arnold, Mavis, 103
auditions, 38
authenticity, preparedness and, 60–3

Baker, Barry, 5
Bannon, Dermot, 163
Barry, Gerald, 76, 89
BBC Northern Ireland, 1
Beef Tribunal, 140
Bernstein, Carl, 69
Big Debates, 73–4
blackmail, 134, 135, 141–2
body language, 128–32
Boss, The (Murtagh and Joyce), 94
Bradley, Ben, 69
Brady, Vincent, 119
Brennan, Séamus, 55, 87

Browne, Vincent, 76, 95, 98, 103, 108, 169
Bruton, John, 25, 177, 178
Burke, Ray, 99, 116–17, 119, 136
Burlington Hotel, Dublin, 56, 57, 117
Byrne, Gay (Gaybo), 35, 54, 122–3, 145

Caine, Michael, 132
car accident, 30, 31, 44
Carr, Bunny, 2–4, 7, 8–10, 12, 26
    FitzGerald, Garret and, 16, 23–4, 48
    media training and, 4–5, 6
    O'Malley, Des and, 146
    retirement, 154
    training courses, 32–3
Carr, Joan, 154
Carr Communications, 10, 11
    corporate videos, 29
    director/shareholders, 30
    Doherty, Seán and, 99–107
    Fianna Fáil and, 15, 16, 19, 25, 42–4, 46, 91
    finances, 29, 31–2
    Fine Gael and, 15, 25–6, 48
    FitzGerald, Garret and, 23–4
    Haughey and, 15, 41, 42, 46–7, 48–50, 91–2

Labour Party and, 15, 26–7
management buy-out, 154, 163–4
marketing, 25, 32
political parties and, 15
political training, association with, 24–5, 33
PR unit, 30, 32
private sector and, 19
redundancies, 32
training courses, 32–3
Carter, Jimmy, 67
Casey, Sue, 158, 160–1
Catholic Church, 4
Catholic clergy, 7
Catholic Communications Centre, 4–5, 8, 9
Catholic hierarchy, 4, 9
Chartered Accountants Ireland, 161
Churchill, Winston, 123
Clinton, Bill, 72
Cluskey, Frank, 23
COCO Television, 134
Colley, George, 13, 108
Collins, Gerry, 119
Comisiún na Meán, 74
Communications Clinic, The, 8, 133, 164
Conway, William, Cardinal, 126
Corish, Brendan, 18
corporate crises, 134
Corwin, Norman, 70–1
Cosgrave, Liam, 22
Costello, Declan, 23
Country & Western Alliance, 86, 90, 91, 110, 112, 169
Cowen, Brian, 139
crisis communications, 132–4
crisis management, 133–4
Cronin, Bart, 120–2, 150

Crosbie, Alan, 164
Cullen, Linda, 134, 163
Cunnane, Joseph, Archbishop of Tuam, 88
Curran, Tom, 166
Custom House, Dublin, 77, 78, 120, 146

Dáil Éireann, first women elected to, 33–4
Daly, Brendan, 88, 119
Dand, Ian, 32–3
D'Arcy, Rev. Brian, 4
Davern, Noel, 119, 127
Davin-Power, David, 30
de Valera, Éamon, 13, 21, 22
debates, preparation for, 73–4
Department of the Environment, 147
Department of Foreign Affairs, 24
Department of Health, 139, 143
Department of Justice, 102, 103
Dillon, James, 92
Doherty, Maura, 100–1, 105, 108, 109–10, 111, 112, 113–14
Doherty, Seán, 93, 95, 98, 169
    Ahern, Bertie and, 169, 170
    Carr Communications and, 99–107
    as Cathaoirleach of the Seanad, 104
    Haughey and, 108, 112
    as Minister for Justice, 102–4
    Nighthawks and, 94, 99
    phone tapping and, 98, 99, 100–8
    press briefing, 109–10, 111–12
    reactions to confession, 113, 115, 137
Donohoe, Paschal, 165
Douglas, Walter, 160
Doyle, Diarmuid, 98, 99
'Dublin 4' mindset, 75, 98, 99, 174
Duchenne, Guillaume, 131
Duffy, Paddy, 54

Duignan, Seán (Diggy), 117–18, 121–2, 126, 127, 148, 150, 152
Dunn, Rev. Joe, 4–5
Dunne, Ben, 19
DuPont, 79–80
Dwyer, T. Ryle, 12

Enron, 79
European Community, 80, 81
European Convention on Human Rights, 126
European Parliament, 65
European Union (EU), 146
expert witness training, 59–60

Fair Deal Scheme, 148
Farrell, Brian, 175
Fay, Liam, 25
Federal Bureau of Investigation (FBI), 131
Feeney, John, 42
feminism, 37–8
Fianna Fáil, 2, 6, 13
    Carr Communications and, 15, 16, 19, 25, 42–4, 46, 91
    coalitions and, 167–8
    Country & Western Alliance, 86, 90, 91, 110, 169
    Fine Gael and, 168
    Flynn's views on, 95–8
    GUBU and, 41, 99
    Haughey's leadership, 16, 18–19, 23, 54, 86, 90
    Haughey's resignation, 115
    homosexuality, attitude towards, 145
    internal divisions, 18–19, 21, 96–7
    Lynch's leadership, 13, 18
    media and, 41–2, 174
    O'Connell, John and, 18, 19, 48
    presidential election (1966), 22
    Progressive Democrats and, 55–6, 104, 105, 113
    RTÉ and, 53
Fine Gael, 2, 6, 21, 147, 166–7, 174
    Carr Communications and, 15, 25–6, 48
    coalitions and, 166–7
    election bus, 177
    Fianna Fáil and, 168
    FitzGerald's leadership, 23
    presidential campaign (1966), 21–2
    tax on children's shoes, 25
Fingal County Council, 160–1
Fitzgerald, Bill, 33, 77
Fitzgerald, Frances, 148, 171–2
FitzGerald, Garret, 1–2, 16, 23–4, 28, 48, 51–2, 98
FitzGerald, Joan, 23
Flannery, Frank, 23, 166–7
Flynn, Dorothy, 45, 46, 76, 79, 83–4
Flynn, Pádraig, 111, 112, 147–8, 166, 178
    Catholic faith and, 75, 90
    coalition, views on, 96
    as European Commissioner, 84
    Fianna Fáil, views on, 95–8
    Haughey and, 86, 90, 91
    Irish language, 81
    local politics, 84
    media training, 43–6, 75, 77
    as Minister for the Environment, 77, 78–81, 120
    ministerial speeches, 81–3
    persona, 75–6, 85
    Reynolds and, 115–16, 137
    Savage, Tom and, 43–4, 45–6
    Sunday Tribune essay, 95, 112, 169
    Travellers, regard for, 76
    women, respect for, 76, 79–80, 90, 95

Foras Forbartha, An, 77, 78
Ford, Henry, 79
Ford Motor Company, 79
Formula Sheane racing cars, 160
freelance journalism, 10, 11
'frequently asked questions', 35–6
Friedan, Betty, 37
Fustok, Sheikh, 138

Gaddafi, Colonel, 41, 49
Garda Síochána, An, 102, 103
gay activists, 145–6
General Election (1981), 23
General Election (February 1982), 26–7
Geoghegan, Johnny, 86
Geoghegan-Quinn, Máire, 43, 44, 45, 46, 53, 81
   ard fheis speech, 89, 90
   friendships, 87–8
   Haughey and, 86, 88–90, 91
   homosexuality, decriminalisation of, 146
   media training, 87
   as Minister for Justice, 87, 145, 146
   Reynolds and, 87, 115–16, 137
   Savage, Tom and, 87, 89, 110, 111
Gorta, 150
Government Buildings, 122, 123, 148, 152, 153, 168
Green Party, 15, 167, 168
Greene, Bryan, 160, 162
Gregory, Tony, 27–8
GUBU, 41, 99

Hanley Pepper Consulting Engineers, 160
Hanly, David, 30
Harney, Mary, 55–6, 82, 96, 146–8
Harris, Eoghan, 27

Harris, Simon, 178
Haughey, Charles J., 13, 16, 22, 27, 125
   ard fheis speech, 52–3
   artists' tax concession, 54
   Boss, The (Murtagh and Joyce), 94
   Carr Communications and, 14–15, 41–2, 46–7, 48–51, 91–2
   coalition government, 167–8
   Doherty, Seán and, 103, 104, 108–9, 112
   donation from Saudi Sheikh, 137, 138
   Fianna Fáil leadership, 16, 18, 23, 86, 91
   Geoghegan-Quinn, Máire and, 86, 88–9
   Gregory, Tony and, 27–8
   Keane, Terry and, 18, 49, 89, 90, 109
   leaders' debate with FitzGerald, 51–2
   Lenihan, Brian Sr and, 137–39
   media advice/training, 41–2, 48–50, 50–4, 56–7
   Modern Prince, The (O'Brien), 111, 137, 169–70
   O'Connell, John and, 19–20, 41–2, 48, 136–7, 137–39
   party political broadcast, 14, 15–16
   persona, 53–5, 57–8, 92–3
   phone tapping scandal and, 99, 100, 102–4, 112, 113
   resignation from leadership, 115, 137, 169
   Savage, Tom and, 14–15, 43, 53, 54, 55, 56, 57, 92–3
   supporters, 25, 47–8, 86, 94
   TV interviewers, perception of, 50
   written commitment to resign, 137

Haughey, Maureen, 90
Haughey, Seán, 49
Healy, John, 22
Healy, Kevin, 111
Healy, Shay, 100
Healy-Rae, Michael, 173–4
Hearst, Patty, 69
Heneghan, Pat, 23
Hibernia, 19
Hicks Tower, Malahide, 156
Higgins, Michael D., 27
Hillery, Patrick, 27
homosexuality, 84, 145–6
    decriminalisation of, 126, 127, 146
Hume, John, 150

incinerator, 79–80
Independents, 25, 27, 28, 174
Industrial Development Authority (IDA), 4, 9, 29
Instagram, 37
Institute for Operations Research and the Management Sciences, 38
interviews, 38, 63–4
Ireland's Eye, 155
Irish Examiner, 12, 163
Irish Independent, 103, 156, 163
Irish language, 81–2, 88
Irish Medical Journal, 31
Irish Medical Times, 17, 31, 41
Irish Republican Army (IRA), 27
Irish Times, 163
Irish Transport and General Workers' Union (ITGWU), 27–8

Jiving at the Crossroads (Waters), 98–9
job interviews, 38
Johnson, Lyndon B., 68
Joyce, Joe, 94

Joyce Tower Museum, Sandycove, 156

Kardashian, Kim, 39
Keane, Terry, 18, 49, 89, 90, 109
Kelly, Barry, 150, 151
Kennedy, Geraldine, 98, 103
Kennedy, Jacqueline, 21
Kennedy, John F., 5, 21, 68, 69
Kenny, Enda, 81, 153, 166, 167, 177–8
Kenny, Shane, 126
Kilroy, Patricia, 146
Kipling, Rudyard, 133

Labour Party, 2, 21, 25, 167, 174
    Carr Communications, 15, 26–7
    Fianna Fáil, coalition and, 168
    'Nessun Dorma' broadcast, 27
    O'Connell, John and, 17, 18, 19, 23, 48
Lake, Jim, 70
Larson, Erik, 123
Late Late Show, The (RTÉ), 1, 36, 145
lawyers, 59
Leinster House, 42, 75, 82, 118–19, 168
Lemass, Seán, 13
Lenihan, Brian, Sr, 27, 94, 100, 137–39
London Clinic, 143
Louis XII, King, 15
Lowry, Michael, 174
Lydon, Don, 16
lying, 65, 128–32
Lynch, Jack, 10, 12–14, 15, 16, 18
Lynders, Mary (Moll), 156–8, 162–3
Lyons, Kieran, 161–2

McCann, Donal, 129, 130
McCreevy, Charlie, 43, 46, 55, 86, 88, 110, 111
    Reynolds and, 115–16, 117, 125, 137

McCrum, Dermot, 154
McEntee, Helen, 148, 172
McGowan, Hugh, 10, 31
Macintyre, Ben, 47
McNamara, Dominic, 30, 154
Madison, James, 171
Major, John, 124–5
Man for All Seasons, A, 57, 92–3
Mansergh, Martin, 52, 136
Mara, P.J., 53, 91–2, 106, 113, 118, 123–4
Markievicz, Constance, Countess, 33, 86
Martello Tower, Howth, 160
Martello Tower, Portrane, 156–62
  garden, 157, 162
  restoration of, 158–62
  tours of, 163
Martello towers, 155–6, 158
Martin, Micheál, 73
Maye, Fionnuala, 160
Meade, Aidan, 154
media training
  attitudes towards, 63, 72
  authenticity and, 60–3
  tips, 63
  tricks, 64, 65, 66
Mercier Press, 165
Mirabeau Restaurant, Dublin, 109
Modern Prince, The (O'Brien), 111, 137, 170–1
Molloy, Bobby, 56, 57
Mondale, Walter, 5
Monthly Index of Medical Specialties (MIMS), 17
Montrose Hotel, Dublin, 107, 110, 111–12, 113
Moore, Phil, 146
Morning Ireland (RTÉ), 30, 77–8, 166–7

Mullen, Michael, 27–8
Murphy, Mike, 118
Murtagh, Peter, 94

National Gallery of Ireland, 54
News at One (RTÉ), 126
news feeds, 30
newspapers, 5
Nighthawks (RTÉ), 94, 99–100
1916, fiftieth anniversary, 1, 22
Nixon, Richard, 5
Noonan, Michael (Fianna Fáil), 43–4
Noonan, Michael (Fine Gael), 102, 165
Noonan, Peggy, 71
Northern Ireland, 15, 122, 126

Obama, Barack, 153
Obama, Michelle, 153
O'Brien, Conor Cruise, 146
O'Brien, Justin, 111, 137, 170–1
O'Connell, John, 10, 16–18, 117, 140
  as an Independent, 23
  blackmail, threat of, 141–2
  Fianna Fáil and, 18, 19, 48, 118–19
  general practice in Dublin, 17
  Haughey and, 19–20, 41–2, 48, 135, 137–39
  Irish Medical Times and, 17, 41
  Labour Party and, 17, 18, 19, 23, 48
  Lenihan, Brian, medical treatment funds, 137–39
  MIMS and, 17
  as Minister for Health, 119, 136–7, 139, 140, 144, 169
  resignation as minister, 143–4
  Reynolds and, 118, 135, 136, 140, 142, 143–4
O'Donoghue, Jo, 165
O'Donovan, Patrick, 179

O'Grady, Diarmuid, 81–2
O'Hanlon, Rory, 119–20
O'Herlihy, Bill, 23
O'Higgins, Tom, 21–3
O'Kelly, Emer, 21
O'Kelly, Fionnuala, 53, 87
O'Kennedy, Michael, 119
Old Railway Station, Dundrum, 16, 31, 43, 75, 95
O'Leary, Michael, 23, 27
O'Leary, Michael (Ryanair), 34
O'Malley, Des, 55, 86, 113, 146
O'Rourke, Mary, 88, 99, 115, 116, 119, 120
O'Rourke, Seán, 54, 176
O'Sullivan, Nóirín, 172
Outlook (RTÉ), 14
'over-the-wall' communication, 79

Parker, Robert B., 148
party political broadcasts, 12, 13–14, 15–16, 26–7
Phoenix, 91
phone tapping scandal, 98, 99, 100–13
    press briefing, 109–10, 111–12
    reactions to press briefing, 113
Playboy, 71
politicians
    Big Debates, preparation for, 73–4
    broadcasters' questions, 74
    FOMO (fear of missing out), 68
    journalists and, 175–7
    media training and, 6, 7, 8, 178
    stereotyping, 175–7
    teams and, 179
    television and, 2–4, 6, 7–8
Politicians, The (RTÉ), 2–4
polls, 22, 175
Potterton, Homan, 54, 55

Power, Seán, 90
Prendergast, Peter, 23–4, 25–6
Presidential Election (1966), 21–3
Presidential Election (1990), 27
press freedom, 69
Pretty Privilege, 38–9
print media, 68–9
Progressive Democrats, 55–6, 96, 167, 168
    Carr Communications and, 15, 146
    Fianna Fáil and, 55–6, 96, 104, 105, 113

Quicksilver (RTÉ), 2
Quinn, David, 61–2
Quinn, John, 87
Quinn, Ruairi, 26–7

Radio Éireann, 5
Reagan, Ronald, 69, 70–2
Reilly, James, 139
Retirement Planning Council of Ireland, 94
Reynolds, Albert, 87, 90, 99, 115–7, 168
    Ahern, Bertie and, 170
    Beef Tribunal and, 139
    Budget Day and, 143–4
    Catholic religion and, 127
    ceasefire announcement, 149–50
    Doherty, Seán and, 110–11
    Duignan, Seán as press secretary, 118, 121, 122
    Fianna Fáil leadership, 115–17
    Haughey and, 86, 90–1, 111
    homosexuality, decriminalisation of, 126, 127
    McCreevy, Charlie and, 115–16, 117, 125, 137
    Major, John and, 124–5

Index

media, interviews and, 125–6
O'Connell, John and, 118, 135–7, 140, 142, 143–4
peace process and, 122, 149–50
Savage, Tom and, 110–11, 115–17, 122–3, 126–7, 142, 148
scriptwriting for, 148–53
Reynolds, Kathleen, 125
Rice, Gerry, 78, 147–8
Robinson, Mary, 27
Rollins, Ed, 71
Room to Improve (RTÉ), 163
Rose, Catherine, 31
RTÉ
Fianna Fáil and, 53
Haughey's ard fheis speech, 53
interviewers, 175–6
Late Late Show, The, 1, 36, 145
Morning Ireland, 30–1, 77–8, 166–7
News at One, 126
Nighthawks, 94, 99–100
Nine O'Clock News, 53
1916 commemoration (1966), 1, 22
party political broadcasts, 12, 13, 14
Politicians, The, 2
Presidential Election (1966), 22
Prime Time, 36
Quicksilver, 2
Room to Improve, 163
strike, 106, 109, 117
Teen Talk, 1, 2
RTÉ Authority, 167
Ryan, Eamon, 167
Ryan, Joe, 160

St Ita's Hospital, Portrane, 158
St John of God Hospital, Dublin, 16
Savage, Anton, 11, 26–7, 62, 140, 155, 159, 160, 164

Savage, Peter, 6
Savage, Tom, 66
Catholic Communications Centre and, 4–5, 8–9
Country & Western Alliance and, 90, 110, 112
Fianna Fáil, coalitions and, 168
Flynn, Pádraig and, 43–4
freelance journalism, 10
Geoghegan-Quinn, Máire and, 87, 89
Haughey and, 14–15, 43, 46–7, 53, 55, 56, 57, 92–3
ill health, 91
Irish Medical Journal, editorship of, 31
Lynch, Jack and, 12, 13–14
Martello tower and, 154–7, 163
moral judgements and, 48–9
Morning Ireland, producer of, 30–1
party political broadcasts and, 15–16
peace process and, 126
political communication, audience for, 6–7
priesthood and, 9, 11–12, 126
Reynolds, Albert and, 90–1, 115–17, 120, 122–3, 126–7, 148
RTÉ Authority and, 167
training courses, 32–3
UTV and, 4, 12
Scheer, Robert, 70
Second World War, 68, 156
Sheane, David, 160
Shelbourne Hotel, Dublin, 168
Sigerson Cup, 12
Sinn Féin, 27, 167
Skerries, County Dublin, 155, 160
Smith, Michael, 115, 116, 117
smokeless fuel, 82–3

social media, 39, 134, 175, 176, 179
Spring, Dick, 27, 149–50
Spy and the Traitor, The (Macintyre), 47
Stalin, Joseph, 47
StandOut CV, 39
Stardust disaster, 23
Stephanopoulos, George, 72
Sudoplatov, Pavel, 47
Sunday Independent, 90
Sunday Times, 61–2
Sunday Tribune, 89, 95, 103, 112, 169
Superquinn training video, 27
Symbionese Liberation Army, 69

Teen Talk (RTÉ), 1, 2
Telefís Éireann, 5
Thalidomide drug, 18
Thatcher, Margaret, 51, 137
Tipperary North constituency, 174
Tonight Show (Virgin), 62
Towards a Just Society (Costello), 23
Travellers, 76
Treacy, Noel, 88, 110, 111, 115–16, 137
Trivializing America (Corwin), 70–1
Troubles, the, 11
Trudeau, Justin, 36
Trump, Donald, 69–70, 71
Twain, Mark, 1–2

Ulster Bank, 161, 162
United Nations (UN), Department of Safety and Security, 172
University of Southern California, 70
unleaded petrol, 80–1
UTV religious programming, 4, 12

Varadkar, Leo, 36, 172
vox pop packages, 176

Walters, Stan B., 65, 131
Washington Post, 69
Watergate, 69
Waters, John, 98–9
Wellington, Duke of, 22–3
Wolff, Michael, 69
women
    ambition and, 34
    career success, 38–9
    clothing, choice of, 35–7
    Dáil, first women elected to, 33–4
    frequently asked questions, 35–6
    physical appearance, 37–40
    political careers and, 33–6, 39–40
    TV appearances, advice and, 35–6
Woods, Michael, 115, 116
Woodward, Bob, 69
Workers' Party, 25, 50
Write and Get Paid For It (Prone), 31, 107, 113

X case, 122